HOLISTIC SUCCESS

HOLISTIC SUCCESS

MIND, BODY, SOUL, & BUSINESS

PAIGE ELLEN HUNT

NEW DEGREE PRESS

COPYRIGHT © 2021 PAIGE ELLEN HUNT

All rights reserved.

HOLISTIC SUCCESS

Mind, Body, Soul, & Business

ISBN	978-1-63730-423-5	*Paperback*
	978-1-63730-503-4	*Kindle Ebook*
	978-1-63730-504-1	*Ebook*

To my mom and brothers for their endless love and support. I couldn't do it without you.

CONTENTS

	INTRODUCTION	11
PART 1.	**WHERE WE ARE NOW**	**19**
CHAPTER 1.	THE AMERICAN DREAM IS DEAD	21
CHAPTER 2.	HOLISTIC SUCCESS	37
PART 2.	**THE PRINCIPLES OF HOLISTIC SUCCESS**	**51**
CHAPTER 3.	PRACTICE EXCRUCIATING VULNERABILITY	53
CHAPTER 4.	COLLABORATE	65
CHAPTER 5.	MAKE TIME TO PLAY!	77
CHAPTER 6.	DON'T SETTLE FOR THE STATUS QUO	89
CHAPTER 7.	GO "ALL IN" ON YOUR PASSION	105
CHAPTER 8.	CONSIDER THE FUTURE DAILY	119
CHAPTER 9.	FIND THE RIGHT BALANCE FOR YOU	131
PART 3.	**WHERE ARE WE GOING?**	**145**
	CONCLUSION: THE FUTURE IS BRIGHT!	147
	ACKNOWLEDGMENTS	157
	APPENDIX	159

The American Dream is dead for the majority of America.

—SUZE ORMAN

INTRODUCTION

The "American Dream" is broken.

And has been for a while now.

No time period made this clearer than the Great Depression. The stock market crashed, and Americans lost everything. Unemployment rates reached their highest point ever. Families retreated to makeshift "Hoovervilles" as their homes were seized, and Wall Street financiers were driven to suicide.

Historian James Truslow coined the term the "American Dream" and argued that the Great Depression revealed not only just how broken this dream was but also how changed it was from its original conception. (Diamond, 2018) While the American Dream was originally a call for equality, justice, and democracy over time it became a very specific and narrow view of success—heavily focused on material wealth, and still meant to be accessed by all. Truslow claimed that the United States had abandoned our higher ideals and dreams as a country.

Due to Truslow's work, the "American Dream" became a common household phrase by the 1950s. (Ibid.) Despite his observations of the United States' obsession with material wealth, this revised definition of success was never amended and has been frozen in time.

If you asked several different people for their definition of the American Dream now you would likely get several different answers, yet the fundamentals can be agreed upon. The American Dream is the belief that in the United States people are equally free to pursue opportunity and that through hard work they can make a better life for themselves and their children. This often includes owning a home and car, sending your children to college, and retiring comfortably.

The American Dream is as much about material wealth today as it was when Truslow pointed it out almost a century ago. The American Dream does not encompass or prioritize everything that makes life great, and wealth is an entirely unfair success measure that sets us up for failure. Material wealth is not accessed equally by all.

The American Dream is—literally—the national ethos of the United States and it is broken. What started as a beautiful beacon of hope has turned out to be a lie.

The current state of success and happiness in the United States is abysmal. Only 20 percent of US citizens feel they are living the full American Dream, and less than 50 percent of US citizens believe they are living any part of the American Dream. Only 14 percent of US adults feel like they are "very happy," and less than half of Americans believe that when their children reach their age, their children's standard of living will be better. (Carter, 2017) On top of all that, only 8 percent of people feel as if they have accomplished their goals. (Schwantes, 2016)

All of this is because we set unrealistic standards for success that allow only limited paths to achievement. If you do not fit the mold you are not successful. What is more, the American Dream has become unachievable for most.

In the 2010s we saw improvements in the United States' economy, but only the pockets of a select few were lined a little thicker. This was not the pockets of the poor, women, or Brown and Black people—billionaires have a combined net worth of $3.229 trillion and their collective wealth increased 1,130 percent between 1990 and 2020. This phenomenon was magnified during the COVID19 pandemic. (Kelly, 2020)

Just one month after the pandemic arrived in North America, billionaires' total wealth increased by $308 billion. Amazon founder and CEO Jeff Bezos's wealth increased by an additional $25 billion in just that one month. While the billionaires were getting richer, the rest of the population faced rising unemployment rates, essential worker exposure to COVID19 with no hazard pay, homeschooling and working from home, isolation from loved ones, a lack of access to basic necessities, and the list goes on. (Ibid.) While the American Dream did not collapse in 2020, the collapse was highlighted—again. Our entire existence became unraveled by the virus. Unfortunately, COVID19 is not the only thing that proves the American Dream broken.

Women today face different financial and professional hurdles than men, many of which stem from motherhood and the unequal division of work within the home. Many women work first shift at their jobs during the day and second shift for their families in the evenings. Women who want to become mothers are forced to take more career breaks to birth and raise their children. Women face hiring prejudice and are also easily trapped in lowpaying support roles without clear paths for advancement.

Women, and those living in poverty, are not the only ones with a higher hill to climb when attempting to achieve the American Dream. Ethnic minorities face prejudices in hiring and pay, with Latinx and Black individuals only making about three-fourths of what their White counterparts make in salary. Individuals with criminal histories also have a tougher time with workplace advancement, and—due to the overpolicing of minority neighborhoods and harsher sentencing of minority individuals—Latinx and Black workers are disproportionately penalized for their pasts and experience higher unemployment rates. (Fullwood 2016)

In a study titled *Rewrite the Racial Rules: Building an Inclusive American Economy* released by the Roosevelt Institute in 2016, the authors wrote:

> At every level of education, Black Americans are paid less than their White counterparts. At every level of income, Black Americans have less in assets then their White counterparts. Compared to White Americans, Black Americans have higher rates of unemployment, accrue less wealth, and have lower rates of

homeownership. But just as critically, even middleincome Black Americans have unequal access to the qualityoflife goods—education, health, and safety—that economic success is expected to guarantee. (Flynn et al, 2016)

While from an outside perspective it may seem that Black Americans are given a fair shot at success in American society, it just is not true. We have made leaps and bounds in attempting to correct our past bigotry, but the institutional ripple effects are far too great.

Home ownership is one of clearest examples of institutionalized racism in the United States—the home ownership rates between White and Black people are staggeringly different. Decades of policies excluding Black individuals from home ownership still have these ripple effects in our society today, and home ownership is often the largest contributor to the wealth gap between White people and ethnic minorities.

Ebony Jones—a single mother in her thirties residing in Compton, California—inherited a home from her grandfather. She felt extremely lucky. Her grandfather was a World War II veteran and was able to attain the home several decades before using his GI benefits. Jones soon realized that the home needed repairs, and she found herself in need of a home equity loan. (Chiwaya and Ross, 2020) It was then that she was exposed to the difficult reality of attaining the American Dream. It is not as easy as they tell us it is.

Jones had great credit, better than average income, and savings in the bank. Upon initial application she was bombarded with phone calls and letters from banks trying to partner with her. However, she was always denied by lenders when they asked two questions—

Question 1: What is your zip code?
Her answer: 90220, Compton.

Compton is a neighborhood made up of 29 percent Black and 68 percent Latinx individuals. One in every four people in Compton live in poverty. (Poverty in Compton, California, 2017) This answer alone could have been detrimental to her loan application as these statistics make places like Compton look extremely unattractive to banks. Low incomes due to the wealth gap and overpolicing cause a spike in crime rates for minoritymajority neighborhoods. Then ingrained racism causes the belief that White people take better care of their homes and are better at making payments. Unfortunately, this is not the only answer that ruled out her loan application in the eyes of the bank. (Chiwaya and Ross, 2020)

Question 2: What is your marital status?
Her answer: Single.

This meant that she did not have anyone to provide for her if she could not handle it on her own. The banks instantly lost their faith in her ability to pay. Loan request denied. The American Dream does not consider bigotry, and because of this it has failed us.

The playing field is not level enough for all of us to take advantage. Skill and good work ethic will not cut it. So, what now?

We need a new dream—one of holistic success, a way for the rest of us to create individual success on our own terms.

- We need to be able to choose our own path based on passion rather than what is deemed acceptable by society.
- We need to prioritize human connection over wealth and status.
- We need to be vulnerable and not emotionless.
- We need to be brave and innovative, rather than satisfied with the status quo.

I am exceptionally passionate in developing a road map for holistic success as I have seen firsthand how unachievable the American Dream really is. For the past few years, I have been involved with a youth development nonprofit assisting teens and young adults with securing their futures. The success through our programming was proven and profound; we have helped hundreds of students realize their dreams and procure the resources needed to achieve them.

Why have we been so successful? Intentionality. Life paths are intensely individualistic, and choices made must reflect that individuality. I have learned that one path does not fit all and "picking yourself up by your bootstraps" and getting to work is not singularly enough to achieve success. We need to be intentional in selecting what we do with our dayto-day lives, rather than accept what society believes is correct. The American Dream is specific, narrow, and constricting. Holistic success must have space for mistakes, route changes, meaningful relationships, and balance.

The American Dream is elusive and exclusionary.

Holistic success is for everyone. If you want to explore and prioritize the other things that make life wonderful, besides wealth and status, holistic success is for you. If you would like to see society embrace a softer side of success that is well balanced, then holistic success is for you. Finally, if you are stuck, unmotivated, or unhappy with society's preset definition of success achievement, then holistic success is for you!

Read on for stories such as Whitney Wolfe's innovative founding of the prolific connection and dating app Bumble; MTV's *Ridiculousness* and *Fantasy Factory* host Rob Dyrdek's early career successes and failures; Brene Brown's struggle with vulnerability; and much more. You will learn of advice my personal mentors have passed on to me and research I have completed on what really makes people happy. Finally, don't forget to interact with the discussion questions at the end of each chapter; either discuss them with your friends or use them as journaling prompts.

Remember the statistic from earlier: Only 14 percent of US adults feel like they are "very happy"?

It does not have to be this way. The majority of the population does not have to be miserable while a select few get lucky with the American Dream. We also do not have to feel powerless to large institutional changes that make finding success harder to navigate. That does not mean it will not be challenging. Creating new societal norms is not an easy process, and creating inward change is not easy either. Growth is uncomfortable, but it will be made easier with a game plan set in place for the process. We need holistic success.

PART ONE

WHERE WE ARE NOW

CHAPTER 1

THE AMERICAN DREAM IS DEAD

Despite being White and male, J. D. Vance—a Yale Law School graduate—was a cultural outsider at his alma mater. He did not come from one of the many "old money" families his classmates did. Conversely, Vance described growing up in a small southern Ohio steel town. His hometown was struggling, and its struggles were representative of many small towns scattered across the United States. A heroin epidemic had taken lives, the alcoholism rate skyrocketed, domestic violence tore families apart, and a general attitude of pessimism had washed over the residents. Vance's family had been a part of these struggles for a long time, battling addiction and poverty while having no access to resources or social capital. (Vance, 2016)

By all statistics, Vance had no chance for upward mobility or to live a materially better existence in the United States.

Vance claims that above his hometown's structural issues—outdated, inefficient machinery and methodology in their steel industry, brain drain as no new industry was moving into town and young bright minds were forced to leave, and low income rates—a strong sense of hopelessness also seemed to weigh down his neighbors. There was a sense in the community that choices did not matter. All people were automatically assumed to be addicted to heroin from a young age, anyways. While they were all raised on the same premise of the American Dream as the rest of the country, they seemed to know that no matter the amount of effort or hard work they produced they would not be able to achieve it.

"That's a tough feeling to grow up around," Vance claimed.

Vance and his peers are not alone. The American Dream—the traditional idea of success in the United States—is dead, and as Vance's experiences point out, there are many reasons why.

Even if an individual does not give into hopelessness and admit defeat, it is challenging to know what choices to make. Vance did not know that you had to go to law school to be a lawyer. He did not know there was such a thing as need-based aid for college tuition. Vance did not know these things because his social circles were not aware either; he did not have social capital built for the twentyfirst century. Vance knew how to shoot a gun well and make really good biscuits, but he did not know who to ask for help or how to get ahead in life as it applied to the American Dream.

Despite his circumstances, Vance did beat the odds. He graduated from Yale Law School. When discussing what made all the difference in the success of his upbringing, Vance boiled it down to two things credited to his grandparents. They took him in and provided a stable home when his birth parents could not. Vance particularly credits his grandmother, who kept their home peaceful so Vance could focus on homework and what was important to him. She also rejected the message of hopelessness that their town had for Vance. She would remind him, "Never be like those losers who think the deck is stacked against them. You can do anything you want to."

Vance also had the good fortune of having the support of many friends and mentors throughout his life from the Marine Corps, Ohio State University, and Yale. They filled his social capital gap.

While Vance has probably accomplished many tenets of the American Dream due to his profession, he was forced to use a nontraditional vehicle to get there. Vance had to find success on his own terms, and he needed the love, support, and connection of the people around him to do so. Despite the lack of money and power Vance's family possessed, he was able to find success through meaningful human connection—not purely by picking himself up by his bootstraps and getting to work.

Vance's circumstances were similar to that of many kids who grew up in smalltown America. The sad thing is that most will not be able to achieve the American Dream like he did.

The Pew Economic Mobility Project released a report is 2012 revealing a startling truth. Forty-three percent of Americans—including 65 percent of Black Americans—who are born into poverty never make it out. Additionally, Northwestern Mutual's 2018 Planning & Progress Study shows that 78 percent of Americans say they are concerned about not having enough money for retirement, and that one in three Americans have no savings.

These studies inspire me to ask the question: Are we set up to fail?

We have had this road map for how to make our lives better by achieving traditional success—the American Dream—for a long time now. And yet most of the United States is not materially wealthy, not happy, and not getting better in either area. Our current measures of success—money and status—breed misery in the forms of loneliness and stress because the American Dream cannot be accessed by all. We need a new dream.

ARE WE SET UP TO FAIL?

THE AMERICAN DREAM HAS BECOME UNACHIEVABLE

We subconsciously acquire the goal of the American Dream through our environments, our schools, and our parents as we grow up. Our schools, where we spend a majority of our childhood, are set up to enforce the American Dream. We funnel young people through our education system to get them to college, regardless of if they belong there or not. Just recently it has started becoming more acceptable for college to not be the first and only option for young adults. On top of that, we are constantly fed the one in a million "rags to riches" stories of traditionally successful people, and we watch our favorite celebrities and influencers live a "perfect" life online via their bank accounts. This all feeds into the idea that we need the American Dream.

The American Dream constricts us to a limited path (of school, college, and career) and limits our definition for success (high income, home ownership, and retirement savings).

While none of the principles of the American Dream are necessarily bad, to be limited to one societally constructed goal is a disservice to a diverse population. Success should mean different things to different people. Some of us need to carry our money home in a wheelbarrow at the end of the day in order to feel successful, while others may want to donate their belongings to charity. Likewise, some may want a large mansion to live in while others may want an RV or small bus so they can travel. All requirements for success mentioned are completely acceptable; however, we have been conditioned to hold financial goals in higher regard. The American Dream—being the national ethos of the United States and largely focused on wealth—causes unnecessary stress for most of the population as barriers to wealth building run rampant in the United States.

The American Dream was not created for access by individuals with disabilities, the LGBTQ+ community, impoverished individuals, those with a geographic disadvantage, those with no social capital, or—as previously mentioned—women and ethnic minorities. Whether it be via discrimination, increased personal life stress, or lack of access to wealth building resources, these populations have been and are presently excluded from the framework.

1. *Disability*
Individuals with disabilities face numerous barriers to success. Often, we default to excluding individuals with disabilities from engagement, whether that is making a physical space inaccessible, excluding them from communication, etc. (Centers for Disease Control and Prevention, 2021) A lack of policies and systems in place to ensure that does not happen don't consistently exist and reasonable accommodations are not always considered.

It is not uncommon for people to subconsciously harbor negative attitudes towards those with disabilities and stereotyping, stigmatization, and discrimination are common occurrences. These factors contribute to individuals with disabilities facing lower graduation rates, higher unemployment rates, and an increased likelihood of earning less than $15,000 annually. (Centers for Disease Control and Prevention, 2021)

That is staggering. Clearly the American Dream is not meant for people with disabilities.

2. *LGBTQ+*
LGBTQ+ individuals do not have it any better. The Center for American Progress released a report in 2017 claiming that 85 percent of LBGT youth report discrimination at school. This stifles enjoyment for learning at a young age, especially if the young person ever feels in danger or threatened. Not enjoying learning makes achieving good grades and getting into college very challenging. The LGBTQ+ population also makes up a large percentage of minimum wage earners, and transgender individuals, specifically, face double the national

unemployment rate. Due to a lack of acceptance by family and relatives, LGBTQ+ individuals are at greater risk for poverty and homelessness. Every aspect of the American Dream is more challenging for LGBTQ+ people.

While some exclusionary physical and policy barriers are not allowed to exist to bar anyone from the American Dream anymore, the ripple effects and mental stifling that still exist in the form of discrimination and stigmatization are enough to make it exclusionary.

3. *Geographic Disadvantage*
Poor individuals are often geographically disadvantaged. Many neighborhoods in large cities possess underperforming schools, do not have grocery stores or hospitals, and are a brain drain with no opportunities to offer those who wish to stay and contribute to the neighborhood's health.

Similarly, rural areas and small towns face a set of barriers as well. I grew up in a small rural town in Wisconsin. My high school did not possess the capacity to assist students with special needs properly or provide Advanced Placement (AP) classes. The nearest place to speak to a mental health professional was an hour away, and alcoholism became a part of the culture. New industry struggled to move in, forcing many bright minds to move for more opportunity. The infrastructure for success is not baked into every geographical area evenly. Some of us have to be scrappier.

4. *Poverty*
Poverty results in a lot more than simply a lack of money. Poverty leads to increased crime rates, lack of access to basic

resources, and stress. Research shows that individuals living in poverty account for the majority of street crime perpetrators and victims. (University of Minnesota Libraries, 2021) Poverty sparks the need for crime (purse muggings, car theft, and drug dealing) as illegitimate income is often the quickest path out of poverty due to the wealth building barriers impoverished people face. These individuals graduate from the worst high schools with no funneling in of tax dollars due to segregated, lowincome neighborhoods. This often leads to a career with no benefits.

A lack of benefits means individuals living in poverty have unequal access to healthcare, leading to skyrocketing instances of physical ailments and mental health disorders. The addition of increased stress within lowincome households compounds these health issues and leads to higher rates of divorce, domestic violence, and selfmedicating. Furthermore, 40 percent of children from lowincome households experience multiple instances of childhood trauma. As a result, they are more likely to drop out of high school, do drugs, end up in jail, and inflict the same trauma they experienced on their children. (O'Connor, Finkbiner, and Watson, 2012)

These odds make it almost impossible to achieve the American Dream and what's more, they ensure a cycle of poverty is maintained throughout generations.

5. *Lack of Social Capital*
Any of the barriers above, or the intersectionality of two or more, often result in a lack of social capital—the connections and shared values between people. (Cancialoci, 2014) Social

capital is often the result of one's wealth and geographic advantage/disadvantage. Early in life, our parents' social capital is also our own. Their connections decide which neighborhood we live in, schools we attend, the friends we have, and often influence the values we will possess. Eventually there is a transition, and you are able to slowly build your own social capital; however, true social capital building does not begin until life after high school. The tricky part is that your social capital in high school can have a huge influence on where you end up after graduation. After all, as the common phrase goes, "It's not what you know, but who you know."

This is a problem because of the unequal distribution of wealth in the United States. Different geographic areas determine the quality of social capital, as it applies to the American Dream, we build. For example, in the first quarter of 2018, over half of all venture capitalist dollars went to businesses in California and Massachusetts. (Soergal, 2018) This was billions of dollars invested into building the economies within these two states. What else is in California and Massachusetts? A smattering of the country's most elite universities. Individuals with the social capital to access prestigious universities not only attain the most coveted education in the American Dream but also live in areas full of investment dollars.

While the doors of elite universities have opened slightly wider over the last several years, these universities are impossibly challenging to get into, especially if facing one of the barriers mentioned in this chapter. The majority of American's will never get a chance at prestigious schooling due to the inequality in our secondary education system. Students who grew up with wealth and social capital sometimes even beat out those who are more academically deserving. This was demonstrated in Operation Varsity Blues, the 2019 college admission scandal where thirtythree parents of college applicants were accused of dishing out more than $25 million to William Rick Singer between 2011 and 2018. Slinger used part of the money to inflate entrance exam test scores and bribe college officials. Singer unethically orchestrated college admissions for students from more than 750 families. (Eustachewich, 2019) Not regular families either—these were the "onepercenters." They had to not only have the means to buy into the scandal but also know the right people to get involved.

These largely undeserving students were sent into some of the most geographically advantaged areas in the country, greatly increasing their odds at achieving the American Dream. Actions like these erect a wall between most of the nation's young people and those whose parents have millions. The rich get richer, and the cycle continues.

It is possible to create social capital throughout life, and most people do, even if they are not born into it. However, even if we earn a seat at the table, most of us will always experience disadvantages. Because social capital is valued so highly in our society, meaningful connections without material personal gain feel less important. That mindset sets us up for failure.

Barrier after barrier, disadvantage after disadvantage, and this list is not even close to exhaustive. 99 percent of the population faces at least one of the issues mentioned here, and intersectionality between attributes complicates life even more.

The American Dream has truly become unachievable for most of us. These barriers make us feel as if we are always just short of hitting society's standards of success, creating unwanted mental anguish.

THE AMERICAN DREAM HAS BEEN BROKEN FOR A LONG TIME
The American Dream equals sacrifice.

In the 1960s in Saint Paul, Minnesota, my grandfather took a job in the mail room at a large optical company. His parents' generation solidified the definition of the American Dream within their adulthoods, and by all signs it seemed to work!

Through an amazing work ethic and cando attitude, my grandfather worked his way up from his entrylevel position to a seat on the board of directors by the time he retired. He was afforded allexpensespaid vacations, company profit sharing, a retirement package that would compensate him a high percentage of his salary for ten years after retirement, and many more perks for his employment.

My grandparents were also able to live in a gorgeous home, vacation at their own lake house, purchase brand new vehicles, and send their children to private school.

He did it! He achieved the American Dream!

My grandfather achieved much to be proud of in his career, but from his peak working years until retirement, he did not achieve familial success. He was feeding his pockets but not his soul. My grandfather and I were incredibly close while I was growing up. We renovated my family's home together, he brought me to every orthodontist appointment, and showed up to each school event, no matter how trivial. Turns out, I was fortunate. He was not always so available.

When my mother and uncles were young my grandfather was never home. He was always at work. My grandfather's job demanded almost all his time. He loved and provided for his family, but he felt as if he had to prioritize his career to do so. As I got older and started seriously looking into careers myself by, as teens do, Googling the highest paid professions, my grandfather would remind me, "Paige, money doesn't buy happy." Simple words, but ones to live by.

Most would agree that money is absolutely required to be able to do the things you want to do in life. Money does literally make the world go round. However, when more of it means sacrificing happiness within another area of our lives, we have not actually achieved success.

When speaking with my uncle about his career progression, as he is an incredibly smart and personable man, he tells me that he is weary about moving up the ladder too much. Everyone in our family knows that he could progress very quickly within his company or elsewhere; however, he chooses not to entertain many requests for promotions. Why? He saw the lack of family life his father's career afforded him.

"I make enough money. I like what I do. Why change it just to earn more?" He was not willing to sacrifice the balance he had found of success in his life for a higher paycheck.

The American Dream is largely wealthfocused, ensuring a large portion of us fail at achieving it. Our society is not built for all of us to be wealthy, and furthermore, for us to be wealthy *and* happy. While my grandfather was able to subscribe to and achieve the American Dream in its prime, he had to sacrifice his family in return. It was not enough to bring him, or the people around him, complete happiness.

We must stop basing selfworth solely on financial success through the American Dream and begin to redefine selfworth using factors that contribute to success in other domains of life, like meaningful relationships and making time to relax. This is not to say earning money is bad and securing your financial future is futile, but rather that earning money is not worth the risk of feeling disconnected.

NO AMOUNT OF "TRADITIONAL SUCCESS" WILL PROTECT YOU FROM LONELINESS

Basing one's selfworth on financial success puts at us risk for loneliness.

Success is addictive, but addiction to success is not viewed in the same way as addiction to drugs or alcohol. (Brooks, 2020) If you were to see a movie headline that indicated the main character had an addiction to alcohol, you would expect a bleak and tumultuous film. You would not have that same reaction to a headline that indicated an addiction to success.

The truth is, according to research, the same downward spirals, personal loss, and isolation that exist in alcoholism also exist in success addiction, and the consequences can be just as severe.

Thomas Joiner, in his 2011 book *Lonely at the Top*, explains that loneliness and misery in success is a result of snubbing personal relationships in favor of achieving financial and status goals. While focusing on success brings joy in the short-term, a heavier focus on building meaningful relationships is actually protective and will bring more life satisfaction in the longterm. If we solely focus on our financial and status goals, we lose our happiness when we do not achieve these goals. This is seen very often in retirement when older adults have not sustained healthy relationships throughout their life. Retirement looks more like a death sentence, as it feels like the loss of purpose.

Deborah Ward—lead author of a study done on the financial contingency of selfworth at the University at Buffalo—claims, "Feeling pressure to achieve financial goals means we're putting ourselves to work at the cost of spending time with loved ones, and it's that lack of time spent with people close to us that's associated with feeling lonely and disconnected." The American Dream puts unnecessary financial pressure on all of us while our society provides too many barriers to achievement.

Success is addictive because it can never truly be satisfied—there is always another task to cross off, more money to make, or another strategy to implement. This addiction makes us lonely.

LET'S MAKE A CHANGE

The American Dream lacks empathy, is indifferent to human vulnerability, and turns a blind eye to personal circumstances and misfortune. There is a great quote by author Dennis Lehane that goes along the lines of, "Empathy is getting down on your knees, looking someone else in the eye and realizing you could be them, and all that separates you is luck." (2012) A lot of us work extremely hard for what we have, but it would be a lie to say that we don't also have blessings outside of our control working for us. No one chooses the circumstances they are dealt. For some of us this means we have it easier; for others it means we just have to work harder. For the rest of the population, traditional success and the American Dream are unachievable. I say it's time to even the playing field.

Measures of success and happiness are skewed in the United States, and there is unequal access to opportunity and numerous barriers standing in each American's way. It is easy to feel powerless when you are unable to make large institutional changes that will improve our circumstances, but we can define and implement a new individual definition of success for ourselves, as well as our own path to get there.

Our national ideals cannot be exclusionary. So, let's change them.

KEY TAKEAWAYS:
1. There are far too many barriers to the American Dream to make it an achievable ideal for the US population.
2. Wealth should not be the sole definition of success and happiness.

3. Traditional success is a breeding ground for loneliness.
4. We have the power to create a new dream!

DISCUSSION QUESTIONS:
1. What other barriers to traditional success (not discussed here) exist in US society today?
2. How might we fill each other's social capital gaps?
3. What is worth valuing more than wealth or status?

CHAPTER 2

HOLISTIC SUCCESS

"Do you think you are successful?"

Imagine attending a dinner party. Every guest has a net worth in the hundreds of millions or even billions of dollars range. And then there is you. You come from a humble background and make a good living but are not on the same level as the other guests.

Then someone at the dinner table asks this question, "Do you think you are successful?"

This experience happened to John Hall, a writer for Forbes Magazine. Hall attended a dinner he honestly felt lucky to be invited to, and then one man at the dinner table asked that question. Absolute silence fell over the attendees; they did not know how to answer. (2018)

"Do you think you are successful?" he asked again. This time he urged for complete honesty and even volunteered to answer first. The inquisitor explained that he was in the middle of another divorce, his kids did not want to spend time with him, and his only friends were around for business purposes exclusively. Hall was astonished at his transparency, but as the dialogue grew more and more extremely wealthy individuals voiced the very real struggles they were facing in areas of their lives outside finance. By the end of the conversation it was clear—no, they did not feel successful.

By all measures of success we currently use, these people had achieved success. I am sure they had few worries financially, but they did not feel successful holistically and their happiness suffered because of it.

As a society we have done away with the caste systems of the past and have called for complete equality among the entire human race. However, as the United States is a capitalist country, this complete equality has transformed our daytoday experiences into something else—a meritocracy.

Meritocracies bring us hope, a hope that is catalyzed by the prospect of the American Dream. Through the structuring of our society, we are taught to believe that if we have talent and work ethic, nothing will hold us back from achieving success—a.k.a. the American Dream. As the American Dream is the paramount symbol of success in the United States, this prospect is quite exciting.

While we are taught in a meritocratic society our success is entirely our own, we are also taught this is true of our failures. If we don't "make it" it is entirely our fault. Meritocratic societies, like the United States, have the highest rate of mental health disorders and suicide because actually, it is impossible to develop a true meritocracy. This is because, as it has been highlighted throughout US history, we are not truly all equal—that ideal is a lie.

A true meritocratic society would have to be created in a vacuum, where each individual comes into the world with the same life circumstances and potential skill level. (Brooks, 2019) We know this does not happen. It is very clear that someone obtaining a large sum of money via a trust fund for turning eighteen and someone who has struggled in the foster care system throughout childhood have very different starting points in our "meritocracy." Yet somehow, both are supposed to have an equal shot at achieving the American Dream. This is not a true reflection of reality, but we have been conditioned to believe it.

There are simply too many random factors at play to ensure every individual has an equal and fair path to the American Dream and financial success. This means some automatically rise to the top of society while others fall to the bottom. These facts mean meritocracies are based solely on competition. It makes our purpose not to be a soul that experiences life on earth but rather to be a set of skills and resources to be maximized throughout lifetime. Possibly most importantly, a meritocratic society makes those with less "merit" than others seen as less valuable in the eyes of society.

We have put so much value on achieving the American Dream and have bought way too far into our meritocratic structure that it is causing our population to suffer with unneeded mental anguish. This is because a good work ethic is not all it takes; the American Dream is not an equitable ideal for our society to teach. What's more is that the pursuit of the American Dream often leads to sacrifice in other areas of our lives that may actually make us happier than traditional success. We need to change our definition of success to a definition that values prosperity in mind, body, soul, and business—we need holistic success.

Holistic success will be a new goal to work towards that, once achieved, will be a better reflection of what a life well lived looks like. The emphasis will no longer be placed on wealth and status, but rather on balanced success in all areas that make life great.

IT'S ABOUT TIME WE CHANGE THINGS UP!

PEOPLE ARE THE MOST VALUABLE CURRENCY
Our society tells us lies about what is important to live a great life and, as you may have guessed, this includes wealth and status. These priorities breed unwarranted financial pressure and demanding work environments. The meritocracy fueling our beliefs makes our society incredibly individualistic and this leads to misery.

David Brooks—a New York Times OpEd columnist and author—spoke of a time in his life he called a "bad season." (2019) His wife had divorced him, his kids were off to college, and he had lost many friends due to differing beliefs. During this time, Brooks lived in an apartment alone and worked all hours of the day. He recalled, "If you opened the kitchen drawers, where there should have been utensils, there were Post-it notes." And, "If you opened the drawer where there were supposed to be plates, I had envelopes." His weekends were spent lonely, waiting impatiently for the work week to arrive. To him, this loneliness was akin to being drunk. He was making a series of bad decisions and living very unstable. The hardest realization Brooks had was when it was clear that the emptiness of his apartment was a reflection of the emptiness in himself.

Brooks claims that he "had fallen for some of the lies our culture tells us, the first of which is that career success is fulfilling." Sure, career success had allowed Brooks to not feel like a "failure" but did not necessarily bring him any real happiness. Brooks also bought into the idea that self-sufficiency will lead to a better life, the idea that the next big thing we can accomplish—pounds lost, dollars saved, car bought, etc.—will make us happier. However, as Brooks put it, "The things that make you happy are the deep relationships of life, the losing of selfsufficiency."

Believing these lies led Brooks to "fall into a valley of disconnection," and he realized he was not the only one. Many other people were falling into this valley as well. Brooks shared the statistic that "35 percent of Americans over 40 years old are chronically lonely." A lot of people in the United States are living isolated, with fragmented relationships, and no social support.

Brooks went on to share a staggering account of the status of disconnection in the United States: the largest growing political group is "unaffiliated," the largest growing religious affiliation is "unaffiliated," mental health disorder rates are soaring, less than 10 percent of people report trusting their neighbors, and more people are addicted to substances than at any other point in human history. To Brooks this means we have a "social and relational crisis."

To get out of the valley of disconnection, we need each other—we cannot do it alone.

During this "bad season" in his life Brooks realized that you can either "get broken, or get broken open." Suffering finds the basement of your soul and digs a hole, revealing another cavity below, and then it goes deeper, revealing another cavity. You can either stay empty or feed your soul with social and spiritual food. Only through vulnerability and connection can those gaps be filled. Those who do not fill the cavities with positives leave room for pain to move in and become broken, and people who take on pain also transmit it.

Once you have fallen into a valley it is very difficult to get out on your own. According to Brooks, "You can't climb out, someone has to reach in and pull you out." People who are able to come back from the worst valleys simply live differently, and as Brooks put it, "They have radical mutuality and they are geniuses at relationships." They not only bounce back from hardship easier but also come out stronger and are happier in their everyday lives. (Ibid.)

Human connection is also the fuel for collaboration and social unity, both required to help repair society as it is fractured today.

Humans have an inexplicable care for one another, but society does not always reflect that. We have pegged certain material possessions with emotional rewards. In reality, it is not the possessions we seek, but the reward we believe we will get from attaining them. The unfortunate thing is that we have it all wrong. Human connection will bring emotional reward much easier than material possession, and it must be a goal in our new dream.

MAKE A MINDSET SHIFT

While we need to reemphasize human connection in our new definition of success, we also need to prioritize innovation and passion.

Journalist Courtney Martin gave a TED Talk in 2016 on the topic of "The New American Dream." She spoke of how in the United States we have become obsessed with "economic transcendence"—the idea that each generation will surpass the previous financially. However, as Martin learned, the current adult cohort is the first in US history that does not believe the next generation will be better off.

This prompted Martin to do some of her own research. She found that more adults are choosing freelance jobs in place of stable employment, homeownership rates are at alltime lows, and we are not making as much as our parents and grandparents in pay. According to Martin, "We are not finding steady employment, we are not earning as much money, we are not living in fancy houses." These are three tenets of the American Dream—three reasons individuals move to the United States in search of a "better life"—but they are not painting an accurate picture of what is happening here today.

Martin stated that what she believes makes the United States great is its "spirit of reinvention." With the recession of 2008 not too distant in our memories, researchers have taken the time to study both the causes and the impact of the recession on US society. By examining this research, Martin concluded that recessions can be the "Father of consciousness" that force us to ask questions we may not otherwise ask like, "How should we work?" and, "How should we live?" (Ibid.)

US citizens made many changes after the 2008 recession. They are waiting longer to buy houses and have children. They are also less loyal to their employers. This was largely due to feeling expendable after experiencing the high unemployment rates in the aftermath. (Pew Research Center, 2010) The decline of employee loyalty has had ripple effects since 2008.

Millennials, the current largest generation in the workforce, are more likely to hop from job to job than any prior generation: 60 percent of millennials are open to new job opportunities. This is 15 percent more than the average for nonmillennials. (Adkins, 2021) Low engagement is the main cause for employee turnover as only three in ten millennials report feeling emotionally or behaviorally engaged at work. Millennials have even been dubbed the "JobHopping Generation" by Gallup. (Ibid.)

While small changes are being made, it is a disservice to only ask important questions—about how we live and work—when faced with crisis. In order to harness our spirit of reinvention we need to make a mindset shift to continuously innovate how we operate daily.

To innovate, we have to challenge the status quo. History is not filled with people who do things "because they have always been done that way," and if the American Dream is plagued with miserable people, we must make a change.

It is also required that we shift from desiring status to desiring passion. As the work world stands today, according to Martin, an individual's work life will never be linear again. (2016) Industries are rising and falling overnight, the gig economy is booming, and there is overall less of an emphasis on workplace longevity.

As Martin put it, "We need to stop asking kids: What do you want to be when you grow up? And start asking them: How do you want to be when you grow up?" (Ibid.) Work will most likely constantly change, but as long as children are able to cultivate their gifts and design a life suited to them, their actual job title won't matter. They will have passion. This will mitigate the pressure from one's entire future happiness being dependent on a single aspect of the holistic individual. As principles of holistic success, we will create the space to constantly innovate and infuse passion into our lives.

YOU ARE THE MAIN CHARACTER
When joining the professional world, what I struggled with most was expectations. I had received a Bachelor of Science degree in biomedical sciences from Marquette University. However, the problem was I had absolutely no plan for how to use it. To be perfectly honest, I am not sure I ever had a realistic career path that aligned with my area of study and passions. I had an idea that I wanted to help people, but what

I really knew was that a degree like mine brought status. People were either impressed I was able to complete such a challenging program or by my future career prospects, most of which fell in the medical field. I did not know it, but I was on my way to getting trapped.

As Alain de Botton—Swiss philosopher and author—put it, "We need to be the authors of our own ambitions." (2009) It is hard to not get what you want, but it is even harder to not get what you want and realize that you never wanted it in the first place—that is a lot of wasted effort, and how we get trapped with the American Dream. This almost happened to me in my pursuit of status. I liked impressing people too much.

As I completed my degree it became clearer and clearer that I not only did not have an interest in becoming a doctor but also would not be able to find a medical school that would accept me, due to my grade point average. I did not struggle with this realization. It was apparent this career path I had in mind was not for me. Thankfully, I had just completed an internship with the Milwaukee Department of Public Health and fallen in love with that work. I remember walking back to my dorm from the internship and calling my mother. I was so excited because I felt like I had found my thing! I was wrong.

Senior year hit and, as many twentytwoyearolds do, I went through a series of changes. The changes were a mix of growing up, deeprooted personal growth, securing additional confidence in who I am at my core, and probably a few other things. I both gained and lost clarity at the same time. I had been accepted to a dual degree graduate program to study social work and public health, but now the prospect almost seemed silly. I cannot necessarily describe the feeling, but pursuing that degree just did not feel like my path any longer. Unfortunately, however, I did not know what my new path was.

Four years of hard work, and it felt wasted. I had a degree, but no plan. I felt like failure. Every definition of success I had set up for myself did not pan out as expected. I had been taught that college was my golden ticket, and that if I could just make it and graduate, I would be set. It may have been naive, but I did not expect to struggle like I did after graduation. I am not talking necessarily about financial struggle—although there was a good amount of that—but about emotional struggle. I was beating myself up internally every day for not meeting society's expectations of success.

Turns out, I was pursuing a definition of success that someone else created for me: high school, college, then a highearning career. When I got stuck at step three, I suffered mentally.

When I realized that I am the main character in my own story, however, everything changed. I adjusted my definition of success to encompass more: to encompass mind, body, and soul on top of my earning potential. As I began to review my life holistically, I was able to allow myself grace. I had a loving family, forged a close network of friends, an apartment in my chosen city—a lot to be grateful for. At my core I was happy; even though I was not fitting society's definition of success. I no longer had to be perfect in one area because, as a whole, I was doing really well.

This is really what holistic success is all about: finding the right balance of success in mind, body, soul, and business so individuals can design and live in a version of success that aligns with them personally.

CONCLUSION
Now is the time for us to change our pursuit of success from the ideals of the American Dream to holistic success. It is not in our best interest to place so much value on wealth and status; there is so much more to life than that.

We need people, it is that simple. Climbing to the top of a mountain alone means that you enjoy the view alone. It also means you have no one to catch you when you slip. Finding joy in the good times and a silver lining in the bad requires meaningful connection. We also need to be fueled by passion and willing to make changes in our lives through innovation. Society changes when a small group of people find a way to live better and everyone else follows suit. It is my belief we can accomplish societal change by spreading the dream of Holistic Success: Mind, Body, Soul, and Business.

KEY TAKEAWAYS:
1. Holistic success is our new goal.
2. We need other people in order to get out of the valleys of life.
3. You get to decide what success means to you.

DISCUSSION QUESTIONS:
1. Up to this point there has been quite a bit of discussion on how the American Dream has failed us. Can you identify any other ways, not mentioned so far, in which the American Dream has become unachievable or undesirable?
2. Name a time when you have needed assistance to get out of one of life's valleys.
3. What does success mean to you?

PART TWO

THE PRINCIPLES OF HOLISTIC SUCCESS

CHAPTER 3

PRACTICE EXCRUCIATING VULNERABILITY

―

Kevin Hart—one of the world's most renowned standup comedians—did not always understand how to connect to his audience. Early in his career Hart was given advice by Keith Robinson, a seasoned comedian credited with discovering Hart at a comedy club. After numerous wins at open mic nights when Hart seemed to be really excelling, Robinson told Hart, "You're funny, but you're talking about nothing. You are doing what you think people want to see. You don't have any substance. Who are you? When people leave, do they know you? It starts with knowing yourself—that's your strength. You can't be afraid of the truth. If it happened, talk about it." (Policarpio, 2018)

Hart was already great at his trade, but this advice was a turning point. By neglecting vulnerability and the opportunity to really expose himself, Hart was not connecting with his audience. They left his shows aching from laughter, but no more connected to him than the next funny guy. Without this connection he would quickly lose his charm and ability to write new jokes.

In Robinson's eyes, Hart needed to make a change and do it fast. He applied this advice to his act and became the comedian we know today. The evidence can be seen in his comedy documentary *Kevin Hart: Laugh at My Pain*. (2011) In this documentary Hart uses his backstory of becoming a comedian in Philadelphia, PA, to develop hilarious content for his viewers. Soon after release, it became a national phenomenon.

In an interview Hart did with *Entertainment Weekly* in 2011, he attributed the documentary's success to demonstrating that he is a real person. Hart stated, "You see that I didn't come from luxury. My upbringing was solid because of the people I had around me. And I allow you to see these people … these aren't stories that are fabricated or staged to be funny. You see that it's real. And I think that's what people are loving more." Hart was vulnerable with his comedic material and now gets to continue to excel in his passion.

On top of staying relevant in his trade, Hart also gets to use his comedy as a space to talk through life experiences. In an interview with the *Washington Post* in 2011, Hart stated, "My therapy is really to deal with things out in the open, my audience serves as my therapist … I'm able to get stuff off of my chest that I wouldn't tell a person in a regular setting." This was true of his intended audience for *Laugh at My Pain*. Hart stated, "I decided to dig a little deeper … and talk about things I never wanted to talk about … I wanted to talk about my dad being on drugs, my mom passing away, and me personally going through a divorce."

Most successful comedians do use their personal lives to write jokes, and to do this they need an immense—some would say excruciating—amount of vulnerability. Unfortunately, being vulnerable is never easy.

Vulnerability is something that almost all components of nature actively fight against. From poison, to sharp fangs, to fur coverings, the natural world is teeming with protective measures to reduce vulnerability. While humans tend to have more advanced practices to prevent physical vulnerability (houses, clothes, etc.) we also work extremely hard to prevent similar emotional exposure. The problem with limiting vulnerability, as seen with Hart, is that is closes us off to connection, and humans require connection.

Connection is so important that neuroscientist and UCLA professor Matthew Lieberman stated, "Connection is as basic of a human need as food, water, and shelter." (2013) He goes further to state that we have evolved and developed fundamental differences in our brain structure from our ancestors. We are "more connected to the social world and more dependent on the social world." Lieberman and colleagues have even gone as far as to use functional magnetic resonance imaging (fMRI) to present neural mechanisms that make us profoundly social beings, claiming connection has become essential to our survival. (Ibid.)

A requirement of the Holistic Dream must be connection and in order to achieve it we must be vulnerable.

VULNERABILITY FORGES MEANINGFUL CONNECTIONS

VULNERABILITY UNDERPINS SHAME

"Connection is why we are here, it is what gives purpose and meaning to our lives." (Brown, 2010)

The above was stated by Brené Brown, an American author, researcher, and professor who has spent the past ten years studying vulnerability, courage, worthiness, and shame. In her June 2010 TED Talk, Brown told us the story of her origins as a researcher. Brown explained that she was drawn to the work she does because she has a desire to make "messy" topics a little less messy. It was for this reason she chose early in her career to dive deeper into the topic of connection, a notoriously messy topic. Brown spent years researching connection and eventually found something that completely unravels it—shame. Shame is at the very center of our struggle with connection as it is the main roadblock to vulnerability.

We feel shame the most when we violate social norms or feel like we have violated social norms. (Kammerer, 2019) Shame comes in many varieties: not wanting to wear a bathing suit due to poor body image, not being able to afford expensive gifts at Christmas for family members, or not attending a friend's party because you still have not found a job and don't want to discuss it. Shame has everything to do with how we feel we will be perceived by others, and the interesting aspect here is that in each instance we are only breaking rules we have created for ourselves. As a society we have set the expectations of being thin, wealthy, and successful, and these constructs tend to cause immense amounts of shame that we have to overcome to embrace vulnerability.

Brown dove deeper into the topic of shame and gathered thousands of pieces of data over six years. She found that the difference between people who have a sense of worthiness, or true belonging, and those who struggle for it boils down to one thing—they **believe** they are worthy of love and belonging. The people with this sense of worthiness all had three things in common: courage to be imperfect, compassion for themselves, and connection as a result of authenticity. (Brown, 2010)

These common denominators were the results of embraced vulnerability, as the individuals with a strong sense of worthiness saw vulnerability as fundamental to foster authenticity and tolerance for imperfection. By overcoming shame, they were able to put less emphasis on external perceptions of their worth. They could then be free to make mistakes and forgive themselves for those mistakes. By not giving the outside world power to evaluate their lives, the research subjects lived more authentically than those concerned with what others thought.

The individuals Brown researched were living happier lives—by fighting their shame, honestly opening themselves to others, and finding a true sense of self. They determined they were worthy, and actively forged meaningful connections. Through this research Brown made the astonishing conclusion that vulnerability is the birthplace of joy, creativity, belonging, and love.

While Brown was able to come to these conclusions as a researcher, the realizations were not easily digestible for her personally. Brown claims she had a breakdown. Her therapist later claimed she had a spiritual awakening. Either way, with a selfproclaimed vulnerability issue, Brown sought out therapy for strategies to practice vulnerability herself. She knew she needed to strengthen the connections in her life, and she needed vulnerability to do so. Her efforts took about a year, and she likened it to "a yearlong street fight." She said, "Vulnerability pushed and I pushed back, vulnerability won, but I probably won my life back." It completely changed the way she lives, loves, works, and parents.

Brown did not have a unique experience with vulnerability. Humans are terrified of exposing their true selves. She took what she learned back to her research to try to understand why we struggle so much with practicing vulnerability and found that it is because we choose to numb our discomfort, especially challenging emotions like fear. (Ibid.)

Being vulnerable is scary, and the potential resulting shame is absolutely frightening—saying I love you first, waiting by the phone for a call from your doctor, or asking for help—it is much easier to numb uncomfortable feelings. However, Brown found that you cannot selectively numb emotion. When you numb shame, fear, and sadness you also numb joy and excitement. We become miserable and only focus on why and how we numb emotion. This all leads to a cycle of disconnection.

To be vulnerable we need to actively fight against shame, or we will never feel connected. Shame has no room in the holistic success.

VULNERABILITY AFFECTS PERSONAL RELATIONSHIPS
I have also personally struggled immensely with vulnerability. Growing up my mother always told me,

"Your business is your business," with a special emphasis on the second "your." This was good advice—essentially she was telling me that I did not need to talk about my or anyone else's personal life. However, I think this piece of advice inadvertently supplied a mental block to my brain where I never desired to share personal details about myself with anyone else. I was conditioned to be fearful of the outcome not only by my mother's advice but also by the environment I grew up in—a small town where it seemed like everyone's business was everyone's business. It was almost hard not to gossip. Getting personal just turned out to be downright scary for me.

Even though I did not know back then what I know now—vulnerability is key—I knew not allowing people "in" sincerely affected my ability to make real friends. I believe this is what caused me to leave high school with few lifelong friendships—I did not form connections with the people in my class. The lack of connection building was not due to a lack of quality in people around me. I loved the people I graduated with and knew they were off to do great things. On paper, I should have been able to remain friends with more of them. However, I was not able to create deep enough connections to solidify those bonds due to my lack of vulnerability. I do not think I truly realized the effect that vulnerability has on relationships until I got to college.

During my freshman year, I met Sandra. Sandra did not hold back. She is an extremely funny, outgoing, and outspoken redhead who would end up being my best friend throughout all of college. As soon as Sandra chooses you to become her friend, the friendship development is in full force. The night our friendship was solidified, we got deep into conversation until 5 a.m. in our dorm's study room. Sandra opened up to me and shared many personal details of her life quicker than anyone else I had met previously. She created this incredibly safe space that empowered me to also share myself. I think this really was an "aha!" moment for me and I decided to take vulnerability more seriously.

Creating this connection through my vulnerability early on in college gave me the person that I would rely on each time the going got tough. It also gave me the person that I would create the most memories with. This experience proved to me that vulnerability is really the cornerstone of connection and connection leads to happiness.

This was also proven to me further in my professional life as a career advancement coach for teens. In this position I met oneonone with high school students to ensure they were on track to meet their goals while in school and for life after. It was expected that we talked about personal lives a little bit, but otherwise I had an agenda of professional items to discuss with each student, and I tried not to veer from the list often. It soon became clear that these young people were hungry for someone to talk to. They craved the chance to be vulnerable.

This was because so many of these students did not have the proper support system in place to fall back on when times were hard. When I created the space for them to release emotion positively and vent about what was bothering them, we were able to develop a connection. After that, myself and the students were excited to attend our meetings and discuss their goal progress. They now had an ally, and even when imperfect I was still available for them.

There was no shame present in our oneonone meetings. The students were free to be vulnerable and make mistakes. Our safe space assisted students in fleshing out their problems at home, issues with friends, and big life choices in an honest and meaningful way. Many of these students stayed in our programs until graduation. Each of these students ended up in some sort of post-high school advancement personalized to what they were interested in and passionate about. Forming this connection through vulnerability helped me enjoy my job more, but most importantly helped in catalyzing the success of our students.

Vulnerability will only do great things for your personal relationships. And creating the space for others to be vulnerable will make their lives better as well. The resulting connections formed will lead to increased happiness for all parties—getting us one step closer to holistic success.

VULNERABILITY BUILDS RESILIENCE
Vulnerability makes us tougher.

Going one step further than general happiness as a result of vulnerability and connection—it can also be said that vulnerability specifically develops resilience.

At a basic scientific level, we know this holds true. When babies are born, they are at an increased risk for infection due to an undeveloped immune system. Mothers of newborns take extensive protective measures to ensure their child is not exposed to any unwanted toxins in those first few months. However, these precautions are only necessary for a short time because as the baby becomes exposed to more antigens (toxin or other foreign substance) their bodies are able to develop an "Adaptive Immune Response." Each time an antigen encounters the new immune system, memory cells are created that memorize the antigen's unique characteristics. Then, memory cells recognize those characteristics during future contact with the antigen and they know how to fight the potential resulting sickness. (Simon, Hollander, and McMichael, 2015) In other words, a child is exposed to antigens and gets sick, then when the child is exposed to antigens again in the future, they do not get sick.

Only through vulnerability is resilience in the human immune system developed!

It is my belief that the surest proof of resilience developing from vulnerability is the case of the patient and therapist.

There is a new type of therapy called "Psychodynamic Psychotherapy" in which a patient, through talking, explores their experiences and emotions in detail. This kind of talk therapy helps the patient develop emotional intelligence by pushing them to explore the most nuanced and subdued levels of their emotions. Exploration is achieved using the patienttherapist relationship as a window into problematic patterns. Patients also explore subtle, unnoticed emotions through the retelling of past experiences. This treatment has proven to be very effective in treating major depressive disorder (MDD) with a .97 treatment benefit. On the other hand, medication has a .31 benefit, and cognitivebehavioral therapy (one of the leading treatments) has a .68 benefit—the higher the numbers here the better! (Barth, 2010)

This is a result of psychodynamic psychotherapy demanding vulnerability. The reduction of MDD in the patient leads to an increased resilience, but so does the ability to manage emotions more effectively. Through promoting vulnerability, doctors are not only treating symptoms—as they are with medication—but also giving the patient tools for how to manage symptoms more effectively on their own.

So yes, vulnerability is scary and seems incredibly risky. The rewards, however, are great. In the end vulnerability will grow into resilience and resilience helps us manage stress better, be more flexible, accept setbacks, and stay true to the most authentic version of ourselves.

CONCLUSION
Vulnerability leads to connection, and human connection is required for survival and happiness.

Through vulnerability we will develop tolerance and compassion for others as well as the mental endurance to cope with our own personal imperfections, failures, and setbacks. Vulnerability can only be embraced by understanding why we feel shame, and then fighting against it to live as our most authentic selves. Using vulnerability to forge connection will be the first step on the road to holistic success.

DISCUSSION QUESTIONS
1. Have you ever left a conversation feeling closer to someone because you or they were vulnerable?
2. Have you ever had a "street fight" with vulnerability?
3. Can you think of another example where vulnerability leads to resilience?

KEY TAKEAWAYS
1. Vulnerability leads to connection.
2. Connection is essential to human happiness.
3. Shame unravels connection, but vulnerability underpins shame.
4. Vulnerability develops resilience.

CHAPTER 4

COLLABORATE

Robert McEwen, banker turned gold miner, was stumped. In 1994 McEwen took over a gold mine as a new venture, but the geologists on his payroll could not find the gold—not a great start. (Tapscott, 2012) His team dedicated insurmountable hours and dollars to geological data, they continued searching, and they still could not find the gold. McEwen was frustrated, tired, and ready to quit, but in the year 2000 he had an epiphany.

"If my geologists cannot find the gold, maybe someone else can."

He published his geological data and offered half a million dollars to anyone that could tell him if he had any gold, and where to dig for it. He received submissions from all over the world and was introduced to many location methods he had not been aware of. For the $500,000 in prize money he spent, McEwen found $3.4 billion in gold deposits. The valuation of his company went from $90 million to $10 billion. McEwan found his personal version of success through collaboration. (Ibid.)

Conventional wisdom says talent is inside you. McEwan thought about it differently. Some of the best submissions to his contest were not by geologists. The winner was actually a computer graphics company that used new software and a helicopter to map for gold underground. By promoting collaboration across industries McEwen accomplished his goals.

Clearly collaboration works, but why does it work so well?

According to Benjamin F. Jones, researcher at the Kellogg School of Management at Northwestern University, our knowledge base and skill sets are becoming more and more specialized. (2017) In 1903 the Wright brothers were able to engineer and operate an entire airplane on their own. The model of the aircraft has since become more advanced, new purposes for air travel have arisen, and certain standards for safety and quality must be maintained. Today, a Boeing commercial aircraft has a team of over seven hundred specialists working on the project—a much larger team than the two Wright brothers. It would be impossible for a team of two to possess the knowledge base needed to build an aircraft for the twentyfirst century.

Collaboration has many more benefits than just the possibility of finding gold or building an airplane—collaboration bolsters communication, conflict resolution, and task management skills. We would not get anything done without collaboration!

Collaboration not only works but is necessary. Unfortunately, in the United States the individual is valued much more than the collective. We are taught that our fate is entirely in our hands—everything good and bad that happens is a direct result of decisions we have made. When these are the facts of our society, why would we rely on anyone else to produce the results we desire? Additionally, the core principles that our government was founded on included a high degree of individual freedom, with little interference from the government itself.

Functioning as a group goes against the foundational ideals of the United States. Individualism has been one of the major pillars of American ideology. Individualism is a source of pride in the United States, but it is hurting teams. We need meaningful collaboration for holistic success.

COLLABORATION IS VALUEADDING

WE ARE AN INDIVIDUALISTIC SOCIETY

Our eighteenthcentury forefathers had a few ideas about individualism in the United States, specifically, John Locke. According to Locke, our society should be one of immense individual freedom, unlimited opportunity for material wellbeing, and complete limitation of government to interfere with the individual. (Andre and Velasquez, 2021) Locke's ideologies were groundbreaking and went on to form a lot of society as we know it today, including the American Dream.

Americans are selfsufficient by any means necessary. Everyone is their own person, and not a representative of a larger community or group. This selfcentered attitude prevails in American culture—placing the most importance on the individual, and not the collective. Likewise, Americans do not like being dependent upon others or others depending on them, unless absolutely required. (Partners Healthcare, 2021) Because of this resistance to dependency, needing help is seen as a sign of weakness and services like public assistance are mocked and protested. This is hurting our work.

Team members are less likely to ask for help because that goes against "doityourself" attitudes—often a requested personality type on job applications. (Alikhani, 2019) Competition in the workplace leads to employees that are less willing to help each other; after all, there cannot be two employees of the month! Finally, we are far too concerned with our individual work outcomes rather than the outcomes of those we are working with. We do not have an owner's mentality in which all work produced is a reflection of ourselves because of what and who we are associated with. An individualistic mindset is limiting our potential results and is a barrier to holistic success.

Human connection drives mutual respect, full engagement, and cooperation. Human connection is absolutely necessary for collaboration, and yet human connection is also not valued by the American Dream because of our individualistic society.

On the bright side, collaboration has become a positive "buzzword" in the United States recently, especially within large corporations. We have begun recruiting for this skill in employees, creating spaces to promote collaboration, and building tools to make collaboration easier. However, these efforts may all be for nothing.

The International Journal of Production Research published an article that highlighted an interesting finding—organizational culture will not trounce national culture. Even though we have widely adopted forms of collective management within our companies and organizations, American individualism will win every time. This is because "cultural adaptation may result in a lengthy process requiring considerable resources, as well as requiring managers to manage complex change." (Boscari et al. 2018) Independence and selfreliance are core values in the United States. This makes them personal attributes that are difficult to adjust.

Individualism as a part of the American Dream is killing our chances for collaboration. As a culture, we need to move towards becoming more collective—promoting selflessness, putting community needs ahead of individual needs, working as a group, and supporting others. We also need to make an inward adjustment to value connection and collaboration rather than individualism.

CONTINUOUSLY ADD VALUE
Collaboration plays a large role in connection and human happiness, but it often gets poorly prioritized. According to Tony Robbins, American author, coach, and motivational speaker, there are a lot of ideas on "What stimulates and sustains wellbeing and happiness, and the thing that does this the least [in the long run] is buying things." (Huddleston, 2019) There are a lot of things that we **think** will make us happy. The unfortunate truth is that most of the time our happiness is only momentary after the purchase.

The root of us finding joy in material things can be traced back to the American Dream, our national ethos centered on wealth. Robbins claims that oftentimes we get so focused on the reasons why we have to make money—providing food for our family, keeping the business from closing, saving for a college fund—that we end up developing a scarcity mentality.

Many of us are so stressed about money and all the things money does for us (food, shelter, entertainment, status, etc.) that we obsess over our bank accounts and cling to what they provide. We feel as if there is never enough and we must find more. This scarcity mentality causes us to lose sight of what truly causes wellbeing and happiness, like positive interpersonal engagement and meaningful human connection. Our individualistic society creates competition for wealth on an uneven playing field while minimizing values that make us happy.

So, what works?

"Really, quality of life comes by finding a way to add more value to other people's lives," Robbins claims. Adopting this mindset can make all the difference in the success of not only personal relationships but in business too. Adding value often comes in the form of collaboration and the resulting relationships built through trust building. Employees who prioritize adding value definitely have the best jobs.

In the 2019 *Fortune* "100 Best Companies to Work For" listing, 86 percent of employees from the winning organizations said you can count on people to cooperate, and 91 percent said people care about each other. It was also found that forming relationships with colleagues results in employees feeling more comfortable reaching out for help or input on their projects. (Wilhelmsen, 2019)

Adding value will not only increase the quality of your life but also the quality of the lives around you, the work you and your team produce, and the environment in which you work. This will all lay the groundwork for developing holistic success.

THERE IS A WRONG WAY
Collaboration works, but building a large team or creating many crosssector connections will not ensure success on its own; there is a method to collaboration. According to Jones collaboration is mixing in just enough old with new, mixing innovation and tradition, and mixing comfortability and risktaking. (Jones, 2017)

For example, take your cell phone—new versions are released at least yearly, software update nudges are sent more often than that, yet the default camera sound is still the same as our previous generation's digital cameras. The developers could have picked any sound to indicate when a picture is taken. They could have made it "moo" like a cow or say "caching" like a cash register, but they chose to stick with the traditional camera shutter sound that the consumer is already comfortable with. This is exactly how teams should be built: niche knowledge areas must be covered, then you organize individuals that are both tied to the core mission as well as progress and development.

Organized collaboration is how companies/organizations are formed. Resources are pooled, talent is found, and each part of the machine works together on a common output. Institutions like companies and organizations are not always the best example of collaboration, however.

Clay Shirky, in his 2005 TED talk, presented a problem. In New York City, on the first Saturday of every summer, Coney Island hosts a Mermaid Parade. People from all over the city dress like mermaids and flood the streets for a party. If you were unable to attend this event early in the internet era, it is likely you would have had little insight to the true experience of the event itself. There were news crews present, but this sharing structure was automatically exclusionary. A small group of individuals with one perspective were not able to accurately capture the nature of the event.

The purpose of the Mermaid Parade may not have been for mass consumption, but it can be imagined that many people would enjoy seeing and sharing pictures of this event. This is also true of other events held around the world. People want to feel a part of experiences like Rio's Carnival, Chinese New Year, Burning Man, etc. This could not be accomplished until an inclusive sharing structure was developed.

A way for individual contributors to share photographs had to be created. In 2004 Ludicorp launched Flickr, a site where amateur and professional photographers could host and share their photos. Rather than create a new career or hire a team of professional librarians to organize all the internet's photographs, Flickr turned that responsibility over to the artists. They added a feature called "tagging," pioneered by de.licio.us, a social sharing platform where individual contributors could organize the content themselves using key words and phrases.

What Flickr created was an online collaboration infrastructure. Certainly not the first collaboration platform or the first to use tagging, but this infrastructure did influence an entirely new format of human connection at the time—social media.

Social media researcher Zeynep Tufekci claims, "People who use social media are either also more social offline; or they have benefited from social media to keep in touch with people they otherwise could not; or many people find fellows, peers, and like-minded individuals they otherwise could not find." (2012) Social media helps keep us connected online and in person. This increased connection not only makes our relationships richer and chances for collaboration higher but also expands our reach for collaboration into every corner of the world. The benefits are endless—increased human connection and unlimited possibilities as a result of collaboration.

By bypassing institutional difficulties and exclusionary practices, what Flickr solved was a coordination problem. By doing so they created the opportunity for increased collaboration. Thinking back to the example used by Clay Shirky, there were many people on the internet, but there were only a few that had pictures of the Mermaid Parade. The problem was determining how to get relevant people together to share their experience.

The classical answer would have been to form a traditional institution and draw skilled individuals into a prearranged structure with shared goals. Traditional institutions, like news crews, were already in place to capture and share the Mermaid Parade. Unfortunately, institutions are, by nature, exclusionary. You cannot hire/recruit/accept everyone into a company or organization. Due to this, before inclusive collaboration structures like Flickr, everyone who shared an experience and also had photos was excluded.

We must avoid building exclusionary collaboration systems to get work done effectively. To garner holistic success, we have to be like Flickr and be intentional about how we collaborate.

CONCLUSION
The US is exceedingly individualistic, and that ideology creates numerous barriers to connection and collaboration. We must fight against our base instincts to rely only on ourselves and shun a helping hand—it only hurts our progress in the end. Additionally, we cannot become engulfed by a scarcity mentality in which we lose prioritization of what truly makes us happy.

Whether you need collaboration to find gold, build an airplane, track down pictures of the Mermaid Parade, or anything else, collaboration will greatly contribute to your holistic success. Reaching outside of ourselves and building meaningful connections to solve problems and create growth is possible—we are not all in this alone!

KEY TAKEAWAYS:
1. Collaboration is necessary as our skill sets become more specialized.
2. The US is too individualistic to value collaboration and group work.
3. Companies and organizations are not always the best example of collaboration.

DISCUSSION QUESTIONS:
1. What is another example of a situation where collaboration is necessary today, but it was not in the past? (Like the Wright brother's airplane.)
2. Has a scarcity mentality ever limited your life enjoyment?
3. What is one time that you added value to someone else's life that made you very happy?

CHAPTER 5

MAKE TIME TO PLAY!

David Beckham—a former English national football team captain and one of the best former professional footballers in the world—loves to play with Legos. (The Tonight Show Starring Jimmy Fallon, 2020)

Beckham says that he has been playing with these small, colorful building blocks since the age of eight or nine, and his wife often makes fun of him for it. She will ask, "It's two o'clock in the morning and you're still up doing eleven years and above Legos?" But Beckham claims it calms him. Among the challenges of being a husband, father, and co-owner of two professional football clubs, a little selfcare in the form of playing with Legos is necessary. Beckham also uses Legos to bond with his children, having built an entire Hogwarts castle for his daughter who is an avid Harry Potter fan.

Beckham has even used the power of play to get through challenging injuries that took him away from the game. In 2010, when Beckham injured his Achilles tendon, he passed the time by building a Lego Taj Mahal set just under 6,000 pieces. While unable to play football, he even thought that he might like to be a professional Lego builder if his football career did not work out. (Sprankles, 2019)

By tapping into his inner child and making time to play, Beckham is able to sustain a happy and healthy lifestyle. This is proven through his successful family life and time on the field. We tend to abandon our childhood self at a certain point in development, but if we connect back with and acknowledge them, they may just be able to help us out as adults. It may seem simple, and maybe a little silly, but whether you are scoring goals, running an office, or managing a household, play is essential.

The desire to play is evolutionary according to Lynn Barnett, a professor of recreation, sports, and tourism at the University of Illinois at Urbana-Champaign. One reason we may play is because it is therapeutic. Additionally, Barnett claims, "At work, play has been found to speed up learning, enhance productivity, and increase job satisfaction; and at home, playing together, like going to a movie or a concert, can enhance bonding and communication." (1990) Through play, we will not only be happier in general but also our performance and ability to connect with others will increase.

Dr. Stuart Brown, head of a nonprofit organization called the National Institute for Play, defines play as, "Something done for its own sake. It's voluntary, it's pleasurable, it offers a sense of engagement, it takes you out of time. And the act itself is more important than the outcome." (2008) As a culture we are extremely goal driven, often having a hard time justifying activities that monopolize our time yet do not have any apparent immediate physical rewards. Play is the opposite of this. In play, the activity itself is rewarding while the outcome is null or takes a back seat. Many of us feel guilty for playing, like we are shirking our responsibilities or potential for upward momentum, however, play is required to live a holistically successful life.

Approaching the daytoday experience with a sense of playfulness is how we find enjoyment in the otherwise mundane, and this attitude helps us get through stressful times easier. Studies show that playful adults experience the same stressors as others, but they are far better at coping, and report less stress overall.

Embracing play has unending benefits and shunning it may be dire. People who do not allow themselves to play may feel more cranky and rigid, will burn out easier, and feel stuck constantly waiting for their lives to improve. Many adults reserve play time for vacations only—instead, we must infuse play into our daily lives.

To develop holistic success, we will play! Play has the ability to bring us success in mind, body, soul, and business, we just have to prioritize it.

PLAYING MAKES LIFE BETTER

COME HOME TO YOURSELF
- A cockroach infestation,
- A relationship ending,

- Actively working through childhood trauma and abandonment issues,
- A soulsucking corporate job, and
- Health challenges.

All of these events happened in tandem for Kara Latta, founder and Chief Fun Officer of The Playful Warrior. Latta referred to this period of her life as, "A long, dark night of the soul," and to top it all off, early in 2020 when the COVID19 pandemic hit North America, she was let go from her job. She had achieved the American Dream, but the financial security that had kept her invested was taken away. It was one negative event after the other and Latta decided enough was enough—a journey of selfhealing to find enjoyment in her life again was required.

Upon interviewing Latta, she shared that she was missing something in her daytoday life—she was missing play.

According to Latta, "Connecting with [her] inherent playfulness was just as important as facing the hard stuff," in her healing journey. Latta began focusing on "Innerchild healing" and connecting back to "LittleKara."

While very beneficial, connecting back to her inner child was not all fun and games. Inner-child healing involves connecting to your childhood self to understand what deep wounds from childhood are still possessed and what you can do to address them. This process helps us reconnect with the reasons for our adult fears, phobias, and behavioral patterns. We repress pain from our childhoods to protect our adult selves. The problem is forgetting pain equals more pain. Childhood pain will always reappear and often at unlikely times, compounding with our adult problems. It is much easier in the long run to shine a light on this pain.

Through innerchild healing, Latta discovered that LittleKara wanted more spontaneity, curiosity, and creativity. Latta explored this discovery by doing one playful activity each day—rock painting, doodling blindfolded, playing games, or anything she could think of to connect to her inner child.

Playing each day not only brought Latta joy and creativity but also deepened her connection to herself. LittleKara was finally being "seen" and Latta started to develop a sense of selftrust and acceptance. Latta started to accept the parts of herself that she had previously rejected and began to appreciate what made her different. Latta was able to fulfill some of the most basic needs from her childhood—happiness and acceptance—which translated positively into her adult life.

Latta finally showed up for herself and her inner child. As issues from childhood always resurface, codependency and abandonment issues dictated her life, and selfdoubt and shame stood in the way of her true potential. Through innerchild healing and playfulness, Latta got her adult self's happiness to a better place.

While in her playfulness journey, Latta felt like she had "come home to herself." She decided to make it her mission to help people connect back to their inner child and inherent playfulness. This led Latta to develop ThoughtPLAY coaching. ThoughtPLAY has a unique dual-model approach in which Latta assists in transforming the subconscious mind by harnessing the power of play to cultivate selfworth, so individuals may embody their true versions of themselves. The name for her company "The Playful Warrior" came naturally as it perfectly represents the dualities of her journey—the resilience required to face challenges as well as the beauty in surrendering to her authentic self, regardless of the world around her.

Through programming and conditioning throughout childhood and adulthood we are taught to think that playing is just for kids and, most importantly, must come after all work is complete. As this is ingrained in our subconscious, we begin to believe that play should not be prioritized, and we lose our childlike sense of wonder. We are no longer allowed to be silly, and we take ourselves way too seriously. According to Dr. Scott G. Eberle, PhD, vice president for play studies at The Strong and editor of the *American Journal of Play*, "We don't lose the need for novelty and pleasure as we grow up." (2012) Rather we suppress the need for play because that is what we are told we are supposed to do. This is a learned behavior and something that we should not subscribe to.

By implementing playtime into our adult lives, we are acknowledging our childhood selves. This will allow us to drop the baggage from our childhood and introduce enjoyment back into our lives. Through play we will be on track to achieving the holistic success.

PLAY IS GOOD FOR YOUR HEALTH
Having a sense of play can connect you back to yourself by releasing the constraints of adulthood on our imaginations.

Playing is also how adults tend to connect with those around them. Playing is creating an experience and experiences can touch people in powerful ways. Dr. Brown explained that social play—whether it is weekly poker night, a sandvolleyball league, or a paintball team—has an immense effect on our social wellbeing and mental health. Additionally, we use tools like teambuilding games to build connection and increase collaboration within the workplace. (2008)

Through play we let our guard down and take things a little less seriously. This is a connection booster. Sharing fun experiences can foster empathy, compassion, and trust between individuals. This was true for thirtyyearold Atlanta resident Wesley Brown, who has found a diverse group of friends through the kickball league he joined. Brown stated, "There's no way I would've ever met any of these folks before: very, very different backgrounds, very different professions." Now they are spending a lot more time together outside of league night, even planning wedding and baby showers for each other. (2017) They have been able to develop a new group of friends around a shared connection and are adding value back to each other's lives.

The individuals in this kickball league attribute their friendship to the fact that they had something in common upon meeting for the first time—they were excited to play kickball! Most people find it challenging to start a conversation with someone in a random public space, but these individuals already had something to break the ice, and what's more, they all really valued the time they had to play kickball together. A banker on the team said that she loves "being able to have that recess time that we did when we were younger and you can ... be free of your daily responsibilities for at least an hour. You don't have to worry about work. You're not thinking about whatever personal things might be going on in your life." For these kickballers play brings balance to their otherwise hectic lives.

Outside of the effects of play on positive mental health and connection, play has also been proven to decrease cortisol—a stress causing hormone—which in turn decreases inflammation. (Chillag, 2017) This causes blood pressure to go down and the release of dopamine. Dopamine is an important neurotransmitter that regulates motivation, reward, attention, and memory retention. Dopamine is responsible for the feeling you experience after achieving a goal, and more dopamine is great for positive mental health. (Julson, 2018) Play will literally make you healthier.

HEADER 2 - PLAY AND WORK
There is a lot to be said of the effects of play on happiness, relationships, and mindset, however, play is also a powerful tool in our academic and professional lives. Play and work are often in direct opposition of each other, but it does not have to be that way. Something that feels purposeless, unproductive, and often produces guilt, really has the opposite effect.

Playing stimulates your brain and boosts productivity. Companies like Google have even implemented "Play Stations" in their offices to encourage employees to play. Play assists with memory retention and problem solving—this is seen in the rising popularity among elderly adults of playing word and number games to prevent cognitive impairment in old age. (Davis, 2019)

When I was in high school, I had a Panamanian Spanish teacher who stood at about 4'10" but wore 6" heels every day to make up for it. She was an absolute character, petrified of snakes, and a ton of fun. One of the things I remember most about Spanish class is the sheer volume of games we would play to retain vocabulary and learn how to properly conjugate verbs. Team competitions, solo activities, or board games—you name it—we played it in that class. If memory serves me correctly, she was even asked by the administration to incorporate fewer games.

I have to give credit where credit is due—the games worked! I was able to learn the information quicker, retain it longer, and refer to it during exams. The games made (what could have been a boring) class enjoyable and helped my brain make deeper connections with the material.

Studies show that even frivolous doodling has the power to help us learn and remember information quicker and form stronger connections in our brains. Physical exercise increases productivity and reduces mental burnout. Furthermore, play increases our creativity and makes the innovative juices flow. (Davis, 2019)

The ability to play gets more and more challenging as we transition from children to adults because we start to become increasingly sensitive to what other's think. Play requires us to let our guards down and enjoy the process regardless of the potential outcome—including potential embarrassing moments. A lot of innovation is lost due to individuals being afraid to run with their wild, creative ideas. It is time we take ourselves less seriously.

CONCLUSION

Many would not be disappointed to receive the advice to "Play more!" in order to become happier and more productive; nevertheless, that does not make the task any easier. You will need to reprogram your brain to not feel guilty about taking time to play, and you have to figure out what "unproductive" tasks bring you enjoyment. The journey is worth it.

It is absolutely incredible what the power of play can do for us, and it is time we stop feeling guilty for fitting it in. Play can help us address issues in our childhoods, create new community circles to interact with, reduce our stress levels, lower our blood pressure, boost our mental health, and make us more creative and productive at work. Holistic success is a space in which to play, and I cannot wait for all of you to join me!

KEY TAKEAWAYS:
1. Play helps you give attention to your childhood self.
2. Play will decrease stress and improve your mental health.
3. Making time to play will help you be a better more productive worker.

DISCUSSION QUESTIONS:
1. Do you feel that making time to play is a priority in your life?
2. What are some additional ways (not mentioned in this chapter) that adults can practice adult recess?
3. Have you ever used play to learn new concepts and ideas?

CHAPTER 6

DON'T SETTLE FOR THE STATUS QUO

Primo Levi—Italian chemist and author of a memoir detailing experiences during the Holocaust—recounted in his book *The Periodic Table* time he spent working in a varnish factory. During a typical workday, he was analyzing the varnish recipe and noticed it required the addition of onions. (1984) Levi was perplexed. He could not determine why the recipe would call for onions, so he began to ask around.

No one could tell Levi what value onions added to the varnish, not even the person in charge of ordering onions. All they could tell him is, "The recipe has been passed down through generations, it has always been done that way!" or, "I don't know why onions are important, I have just been told they are vital."

It was not the culture at the varnish factory to question processes, so no one did. Levi, however, was not satisfied.

Levi tracked down a longretired individual aware of the origins behind the varnish recipe who told him an astonishing fact. When varnish was created thermometers had not yet been invented. It was hard to tell when the varnish mixture was cooked all the way through, so they would add onions. When the onions were cooked they knew the varnish was good to go—what had become a staple in the recipe was really an outdated measuring technique. (Ibid.)

No one prior to Levi saw the potential opportunity in challenging the status quo. Thanks to him, the varnish factory was able to get rid of an outdated, unnecessary process not only for the current workers but also for all future generations to hold the recipe. This was a small change with a big impact. Imagine the results we may see if we question and change more in our daily lives.

Currently, innovation is considered the cornerstone of sustained economic growth and prosperity. Innovation is how companies stay relevant, ahead of the competition, and connected to their consumers' needs. However, innovation is not only important in business.

Our personal lives are often plagued with todo lists that allow us very little free time to be creative, try new things, or learn new skills. We go through our daytoday lives habitually without questioning too much.

By challenging the status quo in our daily lives, we force ourselves out of our comfort zones and into the land of personal growth. Innovation puts us in a constant state of creative development and problem solving. Through innovation we challenge our current circumstances and ask questions like, "How might we do things differently?" and, "How can we make our life/relationships/job/etc. better?" These questions assist us in developing a game plan for change. All of this contributes to purpose. When we feel like we add real value in the form of innovative solutions—whether that be at work, home, or internally—our purpose is renewed, strengthened, and burnout is minimized.

Developing holistic success itself is a challenge of the status quo, but it cannot stop there. We need to continuously innovate. We must no longer settle for what is not working. Harnessing innovation will allow us to solve problems worth solving—like the culture of success and state of happiness among capitalist countries—while tapping into our purpose with creativity energy.

INNOVATION ISN'T EASY, BUT IT'S WORTH IT

SOMETIMES YOU HAVE TO GET SCRAPPY

Whitney Wolfe, cofounder of Tinder and founder of Bumble, was not satisfied with the status quo of connection and dating and would eventually revolutionize the way we connect in the internet era. Wolfe shared her story on NPR's podcast *How I Built This with Guy Raz*. (2017)

Soon after graduating from college, Wolfe went to a small dinner and met the individual that would become the CEO of Tinder, Sean Rad. Rad explained that he had accepted the position of general manager at a small incubator called Hatch Labs where he would be developing phone applications.

As a recent grad, Wolfe was looking for employment at the time and thought she could help market and sell Hatch Labs' applications. Rad instructed Wolfe to call in the morning for an interview; she did, got the job, and eventually moved to Los Angeles to work alongside Rad.

Hatch Labs soon became excited about a side project called Matchbox, a flirting app. The goal was to connect nearby people in a "nonawkward" way. Hatch Labs strived to be different by specifically marketing to millennials, something that had not been successfully achieved by past dating apps and websites. Hatch Labs did not invest in new technology or cuttingedge matchmaking software to set their new app apart from the incumbents of eHarmony, Match, and OkCupid. After surveying different age groups, they found that millennials prioritized a fun app experience over quality of love matches. Due to this, from the start of development Hatch Labs viewed Matchbox as a game and added gamelike features like swiping and rewards. (Abolfathi and Santamaria, 2020) This new app provided an elevated user experience and something for young people to do when bored.

Several rounds of development later and Tinder (there were a few name changes) was officially launched in 2012. By 2013 the number of eighteentotwentyfouryearolds using dating apps grew by 170 percent and they were all on Tinder. (Abolfathi and Santamaria, 2020) This is because innovation in the founding of Tinder did not stop at design.

Wolfe became a cofounder of Tinder due to her innovative marketing and sales strategies demonstrated during a previous project. To get Tinder off the ground, she visited the nearest college and attended each of the sorority and fraternity houses' chapter meetings to pitch the app. At the sorority houses she pitched the app by saying, "College is all about connecting with people and right now you only have access to the people you hang out with; don't you want to meet more?" The pitch was a little different at the fraternity houses and went something along the lines of, "I bet you currently have no way to access hundreds of pretty girls on campus. Download the app—they are waiting for you!"

She had very minimal marketing materials, just three or four T-shirts. She had to get crafty. Wolfe took pictures of two students on campus, dropped the images into the "match" screen, created a handout that said, "Find out who likes you on campus!" and plastered them everywhere. Due to her innovative efforts they got hundreds of downloads and she was thrilled! However, she soon realized that there was really a much larger problem to be solved—the way we connect with and treat each other online.

Wolfe left Tinder in 2014 under hostile circumstances. It is said she was "ousted." Wolfe legally cannot discuss the circumstances of her departure from Tinder, but she did make the decision to sue Tinder with claims of sexual harassment. Due to all of this, Wolfe eventually became the victim of severe online scrutiny.

"The way people online spoke about me, the way both reporters and complete strangers spoke about me, was jolting. It jolted me in such a way that it robbed me of any last ounce of confidence I had." (Raz, 2017) Wolfe explained that she was not a famous person, but just a normal professional. To have her personal emotions turned into "caricatures" in the media was traumatic. She lost all motivation and did not even want to get out of bed.

Wolfe was only twentyfour years old at the time and knew that this could not be the end of her career. She set out to renew her purpose and decided to focus her energies on solving the core problem she discovered—the lack of accountability people online get to take advantage of every day.

For a period of two years, Wolfe said she became somewhat of a "hermit" and spent all her time working. Her confidence could be killed, but no one could kill her ambition. As a result of her personal growth and to challenge the status quo, she started working on a concept called Merci, a women'sonly social network that exclusively used the language of compliments. Wolfe felt this would help directly combat the adverse experience she had online.

Wolfe was approached by Andrey Andreev, who would eventually become her business partner. Andreev owns Badoo—the world's largest dating platform—and wanted to hire Wolfe to be his chief marketing officer. Wolfe was hesitant to get back into the dating app industry. However, with a little reluctance, Wolfe did a handshake deal with Andreev to—hopefully—officially fix dating with this new project.

Once Wolfe and Andreev got their team together, they had a meeting in which Andreev asked, "What is this app going to be?"

"I think I got it," Wolfe said, "We are going to reverse engineer this—women have to send the first message ... this will change the dynamic of how we connect." (Raz, 2017)

Wolfe claimed that dating apps had not yet been created for women, which explained why most apps to this point had a maledominated audience. Men have been hardwired to be the gogetter in a heterosexual relationship while women are trained to be hard to get; men must be aggressive, and women must be the inverse. This sets men up to be constantly rejected and puts women at increased risk of receiving men's aggression. With this new system women would feel empowered and confident while men would feel flattered. Wolfe, through her innovation, caused a complete upset in traditional gender roles to make online dating a better experience for everyone. Bumble was officially launched by the end of that year. Now, with more than five million monthly users, Bumble is truly revolutionizing the way we connect and date online.

Wolfe was able to use her unique skills, experiences, and passion to create a way for millions of people to connect in a more intentional and thoughtful way, empowering and emboldening women in the process. She was unsatisfied with the status quo of dating and disappointed with her online experience, so she decided to do something about it. It can be said, due to the numerous success stories from Bumble both for friendships and romantic relationships, the world is better for her rebellion to the norms.

There are a lot of things we accept as being a "given" and tend to have an attitude of "that's just the way things are."

I am sure that is how many people, outside of Wolfe, saw male/female dating before Bumble. Time after time she was faced with problems that most would have accepted. However, never satisfied, Wolfe kept pushing and innovating until she found and solved her core problem.

At times challenging the status quo is logical. Other times it means questioning the very fabric of our society, like gender roles or the American Dream. Even when faced with roadblocks, we have to continuously innovate to live a holistically successful life and make our world and interactions happier.

YOU CAN'T CHANGE THE WORLD ALONE
People who try to create social change on their own are often seen as extremists, while those who are able to create a movement with a following are seen as activists—we are always much stronger together. We need coconspirators.

Ipsita Dasgupta, a digital media and sports executive, gave a TED talk on the importance of finding a "coconspirator" and shared an interesting story. In 2014 Dasgupta was an executive with an American multinational in India. They faced the problem of not having enough women in their Indian workforce as the percentage of women in their company was only 27 percent. Across the rest of Asia, the number was closer to 48 percent. They dug deeper into what unique problems Indian women may be facing and received great insights from a young engineer. This engineer and her family lived with her inlaws. Very early each morning she would get ready and rush out the door for work. She would then often spend most of the day at work and come home late.

First, the young engineer started to notice that her motherinlaw started to grow frustrated because most of the housework was left up to her. Then, the engineer's husband and fatherinlaw started to get irritated. They expected her to do more at home.

The engineer observed that she spent her entire day with men her age, yet their only expectation from society was to do well in their careers and provide financially for their families. She asked Dasgupta, "How can you expect me to bring the same level of enthusiasm, creativity, and passion to the workplace?" The unbalanced male/female social norms made it challenging for the engineer to feel successful at home or at work.

Dasgupta commented that the engineer was right, and they had a problem to solve. This is the first coconspirator partnership example in Dasgupta's story. Dasgupta, the engineer, and volunteers from The Women's Network developed a strategy to address the problem that Indian women workers were facing. Their solution was rather creative and definitely assisted in challenging the status quo of the traditional household structure for Indian families. They decided to plan a Mother's and Motherinlaw's Day at the company, so the previous generation would have the opportunity to see the importance of their daughter's work.

Dasgupta and her team took the mothers to the research and development lab to introduce them to the medical equipment their daughters were working on. They described the impact of this work as having a positive effect on maternal mortality rates in India and identifying terrible diseases early enough to cure them. The company then treated the mothers to a lavish lunch and thanked them for their role in making it possible for these young women to change the world.

Every mother in the room was proud of their daughter and grateful to be a part of the conversation. Dasgupta was not sure of the impact this event would have on their work environment, but then one of her mentees came rushing into her office early one morning. The mentee explained that she had gotten home late from work the previous night and was bracing herself for a lecture from her motherinlaw. Instead, when she walked in the door her motherinlaw told the mentee's husband, "Can't you please get up and make her a cup of tea, she's exhausted, she's saving lives!" (Ibid.)

This is the second example of a coconspirator partnership in Dasgupta's story. The mentee now had a partner in getting the men of the household to see the importance of her work and role in the family. By working together, Dasgupta and the engineer challenged the status quo in Indian family structures, which then had ripple effects to touch other people's lives and make the movement grow. This mentee now had the perfect coconspirator, someone that changed the way she could challenge the status quo. Someone to stand beside her and help challenge societal norms.

As our world gets more and more complex and we need increasingly innovative solutions to solve our problems, the need for coconspirators has never been clearer. We must stand side by side to effect change. We need each other to find holistic success.

BE A PROPELLANT OF PROGRESS
Steve Wozniak, half of the founding duo of Apple Computers, changed the world by challenging the status quo. (Wozniak, 2021)

I had the pleasure of attending a moderated conversation with Wozniak focused on the topic of being successful as a creator. As the engineer behind both the Apple I and Apple II computers—which revolutionized personal computing—Wozniak had a lot to say on the subject.

Wozniak's father was an engineer at Lockheed Martin. When Wozniak was in elementary school and a science fair came up on the calendar, his father suggested a few electronic projects. They bought a book and Wozniak learned how electrons travel through a wire. This is when his interest was first peaked by the engineering world.

Not long after the science fair, Wozniak accidentally happened upon a scientific journal meant for highlevel computer programmers. During Wozniak's childhood—in the 1950s and 1960s—information about computers was not widely circulated to the general public. At that time computers were not meant for the average person and were a device many people imagined would never be used outside of complicated scientific calculations and governmental processes. The journal explained how 1s and 0s are used in programming language and Wozniak learned all of it. He thought, "This is really easy for a fifth grader." He did not need advanced math to know what was going on and Wozniak was already very competent at the math he did know. This is when he knew programming language would become his own rewarding hobby—his "head felt good doing it."

Because of his interest, in high school one of Wozniak's teachers set up a side job for him to go to a company in a nearby town and program their computer. This is when Wozniak found that he loved the act of programming and wanted to do it for the rest of his life. He then set a goal—"Someday I am going to have a computer that I can type a program into and run in my house." His father thought this was a lofty goal that would never come to pass.

During Wozniak's teen years, he wanted nothing more than to build his own computer, but that was not possible. Computers were entirely too expensive, and the devices were too large. According to Wozniak, "At the time, a computer chip with the memory to hold one song cost $1 million." At the age of 16, instead of buying computer parts, Wozniak bought a computer manual that explained the inner workings of the device. He then drew computer chips on paper and connected them with drawn wires until "a normal person with a middleclass job could afford the parts," stated Wozniak. Soon he had hooked up an entire computer on paper. Wozniak bought more computer manuals and before graduating high school he had learned how to build any computer in the world without actually working with any physical parts. From a young age, Wozniak was already proving his innovative nature.

Wozniak worked to be the best at what he knew he was meant to do—design computers—despite his limited resources. He stated, "I'd give up a house, I'd rather have a computer." With his goal mentioned above still in mind, he continued with his impossible dream of making personal computers an affordable reality.

In his first computer engineering job at HewlettPackard—upon dropping out from college—Wozniak began to put together logic on computer chips. He was attempting to figure out how to use less chips yet complete more tasks with software. Previously, every chip would perform its own unique function. Computers as we know them to function today would take up an incredible amount of space due to the number of chips required to operate at the level we expect. Wozniak started infusing features like color and time to his designs and adding multiple versions of these functionalities for almost no cost. This was unheard of at the time. By programming chips with multifunctional software, Wozniak was on his way to challenging the status quo by making it possible for the average person to own and operate a computer.

Wozniak was accomplishing his goal of making computers cheaper, but that would not be enough. He had to design something that was also easy to use and lend positively to the human experience. Wozniak attended a social club, Homebrew Computer Club, focused on technological advancement. Homebrew Computer Club was full of academics, many of whom were opposed to the Vietnam War efforts. With the computer in mind, this club had ideals focused on social change—namely creating a more educated and connected world. Wozniak thought, "I am good at designing computers, I want to put my efforts in that direction … I want to help people."

Wozniak was able to build a real computer—due to an inside connection at a computer chip company—five years prior to attending the Homegrown Computer Club, but it still would have been too expensive for the consumer. At Homebrew Computer Club he learned of Intel's $400 microprocessor that was incredibly similar to the computer he had built in the past. Eventually, Wozniak was able to get his hands on a new twentydollar version of the microprocessor and design the first computer meant for consumer use.

Wozniak started passing out the schematics for his new computer at Homebrew Computer Club and even convinced his good friend Steve Jobs to attend and see the interest for himself. Jobs saw the potential market and used his genius to determine how to make it more appealing to normal people. After their first attempt—the Apple I—Wozniak and Jobs created the Apple II, which would become the first common household computer not aimed at engineers. When asked what he is most proud of, Wozniak says, "We proved that computers can be human, fun, and easy to use … This put us at the heart of most people."

Wozniak's continuous innovation throughout life changed the world. Almost every individual owns a pocketsized computer they use daily for a myriad of helpful tasks. The way we communicate, learn, work, and play is different from half a century ago. Without individuals challenging the status quo we have no progress.

CONCLUSION

"Don't fix what isn't broken" is a common phrase, often used in an effort to reduce work and mental effort by retaining historic functions and processes. Common phrases often hold truth, in this case

for example, why would you bring your car to the mechanic if it is working just fine? We must ask ourselves, though, how often do we dig deeper to figure out if something is actually broken or not? What slips past us as "just fine," and are we really okay with components of our life just being "fine"?

By embracing holistic success, we challenge the status quo. We then take it further by continuing to innovate and change what is no longer the most beneficial to us. Innovation can happen at work, home, or internally and we must make it a priority in our new view of success.

KEY TAKEAWAYS:
1. Challenging the status quo allows us to fix what is broken, even if we are the only ones who know it is broken.
2. Innovation often means facing roadblocks.
3. Find a coconspirator to have your back in problem solving.

DISCUSSION QUESTIONS:
1. Name a time when you challenged the status quo.
2. Have you ever stopped innovating because it was too hard to create change?
3. Who is your coconspirator?

CHAPTER 7

GO "ALL IN" ON YOUR PASSION

Rob Dyrdek—TV show host, entrepreneur, and former professional skateboarder—set out to create a feature film about skateboarding, and he failed.

Fed up with Hollywood's "cheesy" portrayal of skateboarding, Dyrdek sought to create an accurate depiction of the sport. (2016) A friend agreed to write the screenplay for Dyrdek's film following numerous rejections of Dyrdek's "treatment"—a document presenting a story idea—within the industry. They then found an agent to read it once it was complete. Over a period of four months, Dyrdek would pace in his home and throw ideas in the wind for his friend to transcribe. In the end, they had a completed script for *Street Dreams*. (2009)

Dyrdek received feedback that his vision was too hardcore. Hollywood did not want such a "real" look into skateboarding, and the language was too foul.

Unsatisfied, Dyrdek sought out his producer and friend with whom he had worked on a film "short," who agreed to also help create *Street Dreams*. The film was entirely written, directed, and funded by Rob Dyrdek. The budget was roughly $700,000, but the actual costs came in closer to $1.8 million.

Once the film was created, Dyrdek was unable to land a distribution deal due to the "R" rating. He had to somehow find a way for people to see the movie. As this was prior to the popularity of streaming services, Dyrdek knew he had to get it into theaters. Dyrdek eventually ended up paying the theaters to show his film, increasing the budget even further. He also did a nationwide tour where he physically visited theaters to do autograph signings.

Seven years after its release Dyrdek received a check for seventeen dollars from iTunes for movie downloads. That check was the only revenue created for *Street Dreams*. By almost any definition, Dyrdek failed.

This is not the only failure Dyrdek has experienced in his extremely successful, twodecadelong career. He started a record label that failed. He tried to get into retail and failed. Dyrdek explained his unsuccessful entrepreneurial choices as, "I threw a dart at just about everything ... as a pro skateboarder, I was making enough money to take these rolls of the dice." The lesson Dyrdek gleaned from these experiences is to "stay in your own lane." This is also one of Dyrdek's top ten rules for success. With this lesson he knew he had to invest himself further into his purpose. Dyrdek explained that he had to become hyperfocused on his goals, create a plan for scalable growth within his field, and upgrade his passion into an obsession. (2010)

Staying in your own lane sometimes even means creating a lane for yourself. Dyrdek knew he was designed to be a skateboarder. As long as he used his creativity to cultivate new opportunities related to his field, he would find the success he desired. Through this realization, Dyrdek became more intentional about his business decisions. He created opportunities to advance his brand image—hosting a television show on MTV, moving into the nonprofit space through the "Rob Dyrdek Skate Plaza Foundation," and starting the professional Street League Skateboarding competition.

Dyrdek often speaks of his meaningful family life and career satisfaction. He feels he has designed his life for happiness. This happiness is attributed to the intentional infusion of passion in Dyrdek's daytoday life, rather than chasing each idea or potential dollar that arises. (Shetty, 2019)

Currently the American Dream does not require passion. Instead, it requires work ethic, responsibility, and dedication. The American Dream calls for us to work endlessly at our jobs, no matter if they bring us any real enjoyment or not. Additionally, a sense of duty to family—generally providing for them or achieving more than the previous generation—pigeonholes much of the population into careers that bring them low satisfaction while sucking up all their time. There are several examples of this outcome across all socioeconomic classes. Whether it be the single mother doing whatever she can to put food on the table or the busy executive who never gets to see their family—regardless of current societal position—neither feel happy enough.

Prior to the COVID19 pandemic, the United States boasted one of the highest employment rates in recent history and the stock market was booming. Despite the seeming economic health of the US, people were still unhappy. (Kelly, 2019) A study conducted by the Lumina Foundation, the Bill & Melinda Gates Foundation, Omidyar Network, and Gallup surveyed 6,600 workers and asked them about the factors that matter most for overall job satisfaction. The status of job quality in the United States may surprise you.

Most people selfreport that their job quality has stayed the same or gotten worse in almost every aspect. That is the definition of antiprogress. Less than 50 percent of people feel like they have good jobs, and it turns out that spending too much time at a job decreases the overall quality. Additionally, 30 percent of the US population is working jobs just to get them by. (Rothwell and Crabtree, 2019) These statistics are abysmal at best, and show a pessimistic outlook for the future happiness of the US. We have to ask ourselves, are we really okay living in a society where less than half of the people are satisfied with their livelihoods? I am not. We need passion.

Passion puts us in the position to cultivate our gifts and feel truly at home within ourselves. We have been taught that passion should be secondary to income, but we spend far too much time at work for us to not like what we do. It is necessary we switch from simply working a job to meaningfully engaging with what excites us every single day. Without passion we will never be able to live a purposely designed, happy life; passion is absolutely required for holistic success.

UPGRADE YOUR PASSION INTO AN OBSESSION

CULTIVATE YOUR GIFTS

"Upgrade your passion into an obsession," is a common expression used by Ido Portal, the movement coach of Conor McGregor—the successful mixed martial arts fighter from Ireland. (2019) A true visionary and innovator, Portal has defined upgrading your passion as cultivating your gifts.

Portal started developing this definition when training as a child. He had an aha moment and realized we can improve our skills, but we just need the discipline to do so. As Portal grew up, he discovered a potential problem with this realization. There are two possible motivations that drive how we achieve success: our talents, and our fears. Unfortunately, our fears normally suppress our talents, preventing the discovery of our true potential.

The good news is there is a solution to this conundrum. Oftentimes the solution is to focus on our fears, rather than our goals, by pinpointing strategies to overcome them.

Tim Ferriss—a Forbes "40 Under 40" entrepreneur—went through a period when his fears strongly overpowered his goals. In a very short period of time, Ferriss suffered two tragedies: he lost his best friend to pancreatic cancer, and his relationship with his very serious girlfriend ended. This is when Ferriss was building his first business, working fourteenhour days, and taking stimulants to get going and depressants to fall asleep. (2017) He was a selfproclaimed disaster and felt completely trapped in a negative cycle. This is when Ferriss came across a very meaningful quote by the Stoic philosopher Seneca: "We suffer more in imagination than in reality."

This struck something within Ferriss and prompted him to dive deeper into the works of Seneca. This is when he came across the practice of "premeditatio malorum" or the premeditation of evils. This is the exercise of envisioning your worstcase scenarios in detail to examine what is preventing you from taking action. This is an ancient meditation method Stoics would use to manage expectations. (Holiday, 2014) Ferriss was intrigued, but realized that simply thinking through problems was not a good fit for his brain. This is when he developed the concept of fear setting.

While fear setting, Ferriss labels three pieces of paper with the following headings:

1. "What if I (insert action)?" He then goes on to define each worstcase scenario for taking that action and then determines what he can do to prevent each worstcase scenario. The last step on the first page is to determine what he could do to repair each scenario if they did end up happening.
2. "What might be the benefits of an attempt or partial success?" In other words, what positive outcomes will arise from trying?

3. "The Cost of Inaction." What are the potential consequences for not taking the action at all, now or in the future?

After examining the actions Ferriss was fearful to take, using the fear setting model above, he realized these risks often had far greater rewards than potential consequences.

In a state of pure fear, Ferriss used this process to determine whether or not he should take a vacation. Ferriss thought, "My business could fail while I'm overseas, for sure. Probably would. A legal warning letter would accidentally not get forwarded and I would get sued ... My bank account would crater by 80 percent and certainly my car and motorcycle in storage would be stolen. I suppose someone would probably spit on my head from a highrise balcony while I'm feeding food scraps to a stray dog, which would then spook and bite me squarely on the face." Ferriss's brain was filled with catastrophe.

Ferriss realized, however, that the risks of him not taking a vacation were much worse. "I could easily recover my baseline workaholic prison with a bit of extra work if I wanted to ... There was practically no risk, only huge lifechanging upside potential." Without the vacation, Ferriss would burn himself out completely and his business would fold anyways. He took the vacation, his short trip was extended to a year a half, and he was able to travel the world while his business financed his travels. Ferriss credits every big win of his life to fear setting, "I do ... 'fear-setting' at least once a quarter, often once a month. It is the most powerful exercise I do." (2017)

It is extremely difficult to upgrade a passion into an obsession and cultivate your unique gifts when you are fearful of the outcome. Our fears prevent us from going "all in" on our passion. To achieve holistic success, we have to examine and develop a way to mitigate our fears via strategies like fear setting.

COME HOME TO YOURSELF

Elizabeth Gilbert was in John F. Kennedy Airport a few years back when two women approached her that she described as "tiny, old, toughtalking, ItalianAmerican broads." One of the women asked her, "Hey, I gotta ask you something, do you have anything to do with that *Eat, Pray, Love* thing that's been going around?" (2014)

Gilbert answered, "Yes, yes I do." The women smacked her friend on the arm and said, "See, I told you. I told you that's that girl. That's that girl that wrote that book that's based on that movie."

Gilbert laughed, but she remembered feeling extremely pleased to be a part of something so big. Gilbert is the author of *Eat, Pray, Love* which saw massive success at 10 million copies sold, was translated into thirty languages, and became a part of Oprah's Book Club.

Despite *Eat, Pray, Love*'s great success, it just did not seem that easy to Gilbert. She thought, "How am I ever going to write anything that pleases anyone again?" Gilbert could not see how she could top *Eat, Pray, Love* or identify any kind of win with her next project. This feeling made her consider quitting writing altogether. Her fears almost kept her from cultivating her gifts and living in her passion further.

Rather than quit, Gilbert had to figure out some way to find the inspiration to write her next book, despite its likely negative outcome. In Gilbert's words, "I had to find a way to make my creativity survive its success." Gilbert decided she could only "go home."

Going home, to Gilbert, meant returning to the act of writing. Gilbert explained, "I loved writing more than I hated failing at writing." (Ibid.) She loved her vocation more than she loved her own ego.

When thinking this through Gilbert realized that on the scale of failure to success, most of us live out our lives somewhere in the middle, normal, reassuring territory. Failure launches us into one end of the spectrum: blinding disappointment and insecurity about the future. Success launches us into the other end of the spectrum, sometimes equally blinding recognition and responsibility. At our core we are unable to distinguish which way we are launched. We just know the absolute value of the move—the overall impact whether positive or negative. The only way to restore the balance is to return back to the middle of the scale—to return home.

This is how Gilbert found selfrestoration. After the weird, disorienting success that she experienced with *Eat, Pray, Love*, all she had to do was devote herself to her passion, just for the sake of it.

It is important that all of us figure out what "going home" means individually. According to Gilbert, "Home is anything that you love more than yourself." This could be creativity, family, adventure, faith, service, leadership, and the list goes on. Further explained, "Your home is that thing to which you can dedicate your energies to with such singular devotion that the ultimate results become inconsequential." (Ibid.)

Gilbert was not only concerned with lining her pockets. She also wanted to feed her soul. As a society we are taught to be far more concerned with outcomes than the journey. The American Dream sets us up to work towards financial and lifestyle goals but does not consider our daytoday experiences while getting there. By prioritizing her passion over her traditional success, Gilbert was able to find peace within her vocation. What is more, if Gilbert did not mitigate her fears and continue to cultivate her gift, she would have been rejecting her purpose. Gilbert made room for passion and found her version of holistic success.

MULTITASKING IS THE ENEMY
Multitasking may be the reason for a lot of our professional mishaps and wasted time.

Imagine this—a clown riding a unicycle down a busy city street. Pretty hard to miss, right? Well, not necessarily. If you were on your phone while walking down the street at the same time as the clown rode past, there is a good chance you would have missed it.

In the past, multitasking has been regarded as a highly soughtafter skill. However, recent research shows that it is virtually impossible to actually focus on more than one complicated task at once; some of us may even struggle with walking and talking at the same time. (Kellner, 2012)

Multitaskers make more mistakes and have a distorted view of how long it takes to complete tasks—they almost always think it will take longer than it does. Additionally, it takes time for our brains to reorient after switching between tasks, and we may even lose 28 percent of our day to getting refocused after task switching. This is costing companies and entrepreneurs billions of dollars due to lost time and the need to fix errors. For the pure addition of extra stress alone, multitasking is not worth it.

Gary Keller, in his book *The One Thing*, outlined the concept of multitasking in an example that really puts things into perspective. "We fully expect pilots and surgeons to focus on their jobs to the exclusion of everything else ... We accept no arguments and have no tolerance for anything but total concentration from these professionals." (Keller, 2012) Any semblance of a distraction witnessed would instantly discredit the quality of their work. You expect nothing but laser focus.

Even if you are not a pilot, surgeon, or of a similar profession, why would you value the daytoday activities that you do any less? Doesn't your work also deserve your full focus?

Becoming hyperfocused on your goals and upgrading your passion into an obsession has no room for multitasking.

Every single person is forced to divide their time between personal priorities. Very few individuals have time that is entirely their own, making free time a hot commodity. Each new activity added that monopolizes even a minute more of your time must contribute to your definition of holistic success. Furthermore, these activities should not leave much necessity for multitasking. There are some things we simply cannot and should not cut out of our lives, so we must add to our plates intentionally.

Ever hear the phrase, "If you are good at everything you will never be great at anything"? Honing in on our passion and cultivating our gifts will never be achieved if we do not go "all in." We live in a world of extremely multitalented people with numerous side hustles, hobbies, and projects. The difference between those who find success within their passion and those who do not, is upgrading passion into an obsession.

DON'T GET TRAPPED
While becoming obsessed with your passion has its benefits, it does not come without its risks. It can be a slippery slope. On one hand, the individual receives purpose and direction. On the other hand, they may turn on autopilot and work tirelessly towards goals they no longer personally align with. The aim is to keep an automated directive without losing conscious control of the process.

This process control can take trial and error. However, by overcoming our fears, coming "home" to ourselves, and cultivating our gifts, we will be able to live with passion daily.

We should ask ourselves: What would happen if we made a change and prioritized passion in our careers rather than simply a paycheck? The answer is, simply put, we would be happier. To find holistic success we must make passion a priority.

KEY TAKEAWAYS:
1. Passion is > a paycheck.
2. Fear will prevent you from cultivating your gifts.
3. Multitasking leads to failure.

DISCUSSION QUESTIONS:
1. What are you afraid of, that is keeping you from taking the next step towards your goals?
2. What is "going home" for you?
3. What other seemingly easy tasks could be undermined by multitasking?

CHAPTER 8

CONSIDER THE FUTURE DAILY

"How did you come here today, who drove [a car]?" Professor J. Rod Franklin, PhD, asked his audience at Kühne Logistics University in Hamburg, Germany. (2016) Several members of the audience raised their hands in response.

"What is your car doing now?" Franklin followed up inquisitively. The audience giggled, but he pressed the question. "Is it having fun, eyeing the Alfa Romeo in the parking lot?" He then went on to ask, "How many of you drive to work? What is your car doing then?" Again, the audience giggled, unable to develop responses to the questioning.

Franklin went on to explain that our vehicles tend to be our most, or second most, valuable asset. Yet an automobile, on average, is only operated for 5 percent of its operating life. We use it, park it, and forget about it—out of habit. Is this really the best system: investing thousands of dollars into a vehicle that not only loses value over its lifetime but also is not used that often either?

Franklin stated he asked these specific questions because he wants the audience to "think as opposed to follow habits" because if we are going to solve our personal or societal problems, we cannot follow the same thinking patterns we do today. Our habits are solutions of yesterday and the resulting failures will continue to occur if we do not start planning for tomorrow.

An example Franklin shared is the housing crisis. "We have problems in finding housing that's affordable for people, yet we don't have problems in finding space for office buildings." (Ibid.) Office space is typically empty outside of working hours, a lot of work can now be completed remotely, and space is wasted on colleagues who travel often. If we change our historical view of "going into the office" we can use those downtown buildings for housing and community development. Of course we could pinpoint issues in that solution, but working against our habits will open us up to the possibility of different and better futures.

Taking success into your own hands via holistic success does not mean planning for the future should be taken any less seriously. However, planning for one's individual future is not the only kind of planning we need to accomplish. In holistic success, we must consider the future daily and make decisions that safeguard the health of society for not only the present but also future generations.

IT'S OUR RESPONSIBILITY TO MAKE THE FUTURE A BETTER PLACE

MOST PROBLEMS AREN'T SOLVED IN THE SHORT TERM
"We have a lot of problems we are facing, these are civilizational scale problems," claimed futurist Ari Wallach in his 2016 TED talk. In agreement with Franklin, Wallach states we cannot solve these problems using the same mental methods we are conditioned to using. "Shorttermism," as Wallach put it, "has pervaded every nook and cranny of our reality," and has blinded us to the more distant future. For example, shorttermism causes us to do things like cut costs on safety equipment and training time, saving us dollars in the present but costing us—potentially someone's life—in the future. We simply are not thinking far enough into the future to analyze the full impact of our consequences.

To take it a step further, "We take people who are fleeing their wartorn country, and we go after them. We take lowlevel drug offenders, and we put them away for life. And then we build McMansions without even thinking about how people are going to get between them and their job. It's a quick buck." Each of the examples Wallach lists has seemingly positive consequences in the short term. Take the example of the lowlevel drug offender: we take a "seemingly criminal" individual off the streets now but cost taxpayers millions in the long run.

With shortterm thinking, everything is happening in the present, both benefits and consequences. But it does not actually work that way—the decisions we make will have a resounding impact on the future, and so we must think in the longer term.

Now of course, there are shortterm, technical solutions to the problems we create, but that is how our problems remain problems. Wallach calls these solutions "sandbag strategies." Picture a home built in an area prone to flooding with the homeowners aware a storm is coming. The nearby dam is broken, as no dollars are funneled into the infrastructure. The homeowners surround their home with sandbags to prevent water damage. It works; the storm comes, the water levels rise, the home does not flood, and the water levels fall. This process is then repeated storm after storm.

Notice the issue here? No problems were actually solved. Instead, a quick fix that can be repeated was implemented. Someday the sandbags will not be enough and the time to solve the problem will have passed.

Wallach instead believes we need to practice a method of thinking called "longpath." This is a process in which you have to adjust three ways we currently think, the first of which is "Transgenerational thinking." We are taught that how we measure whether we are virtuous or good is based off a single lifespan. Many philosophers dedicated their life's work to this subject—how to measure a person's virtue between birth and death. What some philosophers failed to see is that the impacts of our actions are not only felt while we are alive. We all carry a legacy, and our legacy has an impact on the people that come after us.

The second type of thinking is "Futures thinking." This is not six months from now, but ten to fifteen years in the future. Currently, society tends to frame all future thinking from a technological lens. This is not an unusual mental practice as it is not uncommon for certain periods of time to have a dominant lens for how they see the future. From ancient Rome, to the Mayans, to the medieval Catholic Church, this has always been the case.

The issue with our current lens is our problems have become so big we cannot think everything through with technology. This is why Wallach no longer "talks about the future, but futures." This creates an opportunity to open the conversation up to all possibilities, rather than just one.

The third is "Telos thinking." The word "telos" is Greek in origin and means "ultimate purpose or aim." Problems are not solved without a picture of what life without the problem will look like. We are often very easily able to identify problems, and maybe even potential solutions, but we do not always connect those two things back to what we want our final outcome to be. If the outcome is undefined, we lose our directive and limit our ability to create positive, collaborative change.

We are often much too passive about the future. As Wallach stated, "We treat it like a noun. It's not. It's a verb. It requires action. It requires us to push into it. It's not this thing that washes over us." (Ibid.) Holistic success is meant to solve the problem of how we define success in the United States. To change the definition, we have to be intentional with the decisions we make now so society reflects positive changes for future generations. We have to shake our shortterm thinking to plan for our personal futures, assist in solving our society's problems, and make holistic success our new dream.

BE A CHANGE MAKER

"Every science fiction writer has a story about when the future arrived too soon," stated Charlie Jane Anders, American scifi novelist. (Anders, 2019) She shared an example of a story she had written about the government using drones to kill people. This felt like an improbable future fantasy that would never come to reality in her lifetime. But sure enough, when her story was officially published, these methods of warfare were already in use.

As Anders put it, there are cycles in time where social change and technological advancement feed off each other. One very clear example of this is the Enlightenment period of the eighteenth century. During this time there was a new emphasis placed on the scientific method and what we could learn from it, as well as an appeal to rationalization, progressivism, openness, and religious tolerance. The Enlightenment was a major turning point in Western civilization that caused the Dark Ages to become a memory.

We are experiencing something similar today. Social change and technology are feeding off each other, so much so that we do not have a clear picture of what society will look like in the future, even just a few years from now. Anders recalled that in the 1980s, when she was a child, people had a clear vision of what the future looked like. They expected neon megacities, flying cars, and robots. While they were a little off, they were still able to make predictions as to what the future held. At the rate society is changing today, we no longer have that luxury. Predictions are much more challenging.

The unfortunate thing is, according to Anders, people have "become obsessed with apocalypses," and that may be somewhat due to our outlook not being stellar. Climate change has been a topic of discussion for years, public infrastructure is failing, and we do not seem equipped to handle unexpected challenges, like COVID19. This often means the predictions of the future we do make are abysmal in nature, and this makes us afraid to think about what is coming next.

As a sci-fi writer whose stories often take place in the distant future, Anders finds imagining the future an empowering exercise. "Imagining" being the key word here, because as Anders states, "You don't predict the future; you imagine the future."

Anders keeps a good understanding of technological trends and is also deeply interested in human behavior, especially why people have reacted the way they have to events throughout history. She combines these two assets with imagination to create pictures of futures that occur even centuries from now. When designing this future world, Anders does not automatically make it an extension of the present.

By not forcing present circumstances on the future, we open the possibility to innovating, solving problems, and creating progress. As Anders stated, "The first step to finding [the] way forward is to let your imagination run free." Bill Gates has adopted this thinking. If you think about the sewer system in the United States, our waste is essentially mixed with rainwater and then dumped in the ocean along with toilet paper and anything else we throw into the mix. Not a very sustainable solution. Currently, Gates and other tech leaders are trying to create a new system with the goal of revolutionizing sanitation standards, reducing the need for water and electricity, and improving global health outcomes. It is very possible a generation from now will not recognize our presentday toilet. (Bill & Melinda Gates Foundation, 2021) And this is where these individuals take it one step forward, from imagining the future to creating it—true change makers.

I was able to speak to a few change makers while planning an event for the Women's Fund of Greater Milwaukee, one of which was Meghan Duggan—US Olympic gold medalist for the women's ice hockey team. Duggan led a groundbreaking movement to boycott the 2017 world championships if USA Hockey did not agree to increase their wages and support for the women's team.

Members of the women's USA hockey team did not make a living wage, yet hockey monopolized their entire lives, making external employment impossible. Additionally, more support for career development was provided to the men's team, leaving the women's team members fewer paths for advancement. This was not acceptable to Duggan. She envisioned a better future. The boycott led by Duggan paid off and USA Hockey agreed to provide pay, travel, and insurance provisions equal to the men's team, as well as establish the Women's High Performance Advisory Group to advance hockey at youth levels for girls.

Because Duggan was able to imagine a more equitable future, she was able to solve problems that threatened her livelihood. Her vision has now inspired and assisted leaders from the women's soccer team to also take action to gain *égalité*.

Future thinkers and change makers like Duggan have the ability to help shape a better future.

THINK ABOUT THE FUTURE, LIVE IN THE PRESENT
It is extremely easy to get caught "living" in the future. Envisioning and planning for the future is absolutely essential to solving the problems we currently face and create the life we desire. However, it is also necessary to be aware of the present as this is where we find our daytoday happiness, gratitude, and peace.

I got lost living in the future from time to time while I was in undergraduate studies. Attaining a degree is not easy. It requires a lot of discipline, hard work, and money. I remember struggling through my hardest semester at Marquette University. I was taking the lowest number of credits required to remain a fulltime student (three of the credits were even an internship, not an actual class) and yet I was constantly swamped with studying and exams, and my grades just good enough to pass. I really hated my daytoday experience and could only dream of what life would be like once I got that degree in my hands.

Then Marquette raised its tuition. Between financial aid, scholarships, student loans, and parttime jobs, I had just gotten enough dollars to cover the bill prior to the increase. I had no idea where I was going to find the extra few thousand dollars I needed, so I called my mom. She did not know where we were going to find it either, and we had to prepare for the possibility that I would have to transfer to a more affordable institution. I was absolutely devastated. I can still remember crying in the bottom bunk of my dorm room because that conversation felt like the beginning to an end. And it was in this moment I realized I had lost my gratitude.

I was fortunate enough to attend a wonderful university with access to an extremely highquality education, but I was hating my life because it was challenging. Thankfully, I was able to set up a plan with Marquette and remain enrolled, but I also renewed my gratitude and appreciation for my current circumstances. I was so fortunate to be where I was, but the idea of the future made me blind. We will have to find a way to balance future planning and present living in holistic success.

CONCLUSION

In our new dream, we are taking success into our own hands. We are doing the same for our futures and the betterment for future generations. Time is not something that should wash over us passively until we hit the finish line. We must be more methodical in our thinking and decision making if we truly want to implement a better future for all of us.

In reality, our future is not going to be a horror movie or heaven on Earth. It is going to be somewhere in the middle. What is more, our actions have direct impact on what the future holds. It is our responsibility to enact decisions that bring about the best for not only ourselves but also those around and after us. Holistic success requires us to imagine and create a better a future.

KEY TAKEAWAYS:
1. We have to think rather than blindly follow habits.
2. The state of the future is our responsibility.
3. It is possible to become trapped "living in the future."

DISCUSSION QUESTIONS:
1. Can you identify any habits you blindly follow that may be negatively impacting your future?
2. We discussed transportation and the sewer system as needing improvements, in this chapter. Can you envision any solutions to other problems you see in society today that may bring a brighter future?
3. Name a time when you got stuck "living in the future" and lost your happiness, gratitude, or peace.

CHAPTER 9

FIND THE RIGHT BALANCE FOR YOU

Achieving lifestyle balance in holistic success must be intensely individualized.

When I was working on my undergraduate degree at Marquette University, I—along with most of my classmates—was in awe of a professor named Dr. William Cullinan. Dr. Cullinan was the chair of the department of biomedical sciences, led a neuroscience research program, and taught my anatomy class. I swear he is one of the most intelligent individuals I have ever come in contact with, and the kindness he radiated was extremely comforting.

The reason we were all so amazed by Dr. Cullinan is because despite his numerous responsibilities at Marquette, he still prioritized making it home for dinner each evening while his daughters were young. He then often went back to the university to finish his work. Dr. Cullinan was not only an incredible academic but also a loving father.

Dr. Cullinan had achieved a very traditional version of worklife balance. He had a fulltime job he was invested in and passionate about, and he also made it a point to prioritize his family. Dr. Cullinan was able to achieve this balance for both internal and external reasons. His employment allowed him to go home for dinner, and he had the discipline to return to work after family time. However, achieving worklife balance does not look the same for everyone. Outside of traditional balance, there is also worklife integration and living offbalance on purpose.

Having a proper sense of balance reduces stress and burnout while improving mental health. This makes us more productive employees and increases engagement at home. Additionally, balance improves relationships as it requires us to invest time holistically—meaning we develop deeper relationships not only at work but also with family and friends. Balance enables us to be more present in daily life and limits distraction in the form of overwhelming thoughts. On top of all that, practicing balance makes us feel more fulfilled, happier, and successful. (Moulder, 2021)

It is imperative we find the right kind of balance for ourselves.

MAYBE TRADITIONAL BALANCE ISN'T THE ANSWER

WORKLIFE INTEGRATION

For some worklife balance is not about balance at all. It is about integration. According to Michael Walters—president of Studio503, a strategic account management firm—there is no such thing as worklife balance. In his 2017 TEDx Talk

"The Fallacy of the Work Life Balance", Walters asked the audience two questions. He asked, "If you get a raise or a promotion at work, does it affect your life?" The audience members all nodded their heads in agreement. He then asked, "If you lose a loved one, get in a car accident, have a baby, does it affect your work?" Again, the audience agreed. Walters was demonstrating that it is entirely too difficult to separate work and life, and if you cannot separate the two you cannot balance them.

When we are stressed and overwhelmed, we begin to examine our lives to figure out what the problem is. We take inventory of all our responsibilities and try to identify the culprit causing our unhappiness. We do not tend to pinpoint our families, friends, or faith as items we need to cut out from our daytoday life—what we tend to single out is work. When we do this, we officially mentally separate life from work.

This causes us to inflate work into a larger problem internally as we have officially identified it as the enemy. We then begin to have thoughts that if we just worked less or managed our time more effectively, then we would have less stress and we would be happier. Unfortunately, simply working less or better does not solve our problems. Eventually something else will be identified as the enemy and the cycle continues.

According to Walters, what we need is a total shift in focus. Rather than separating things and trying to juggle them all individually, we need to accept that everything is interconnected. This will be accepting that we are "one holistic self" and through this acceptance, we will be able to experience four personal transformations. These transformations play a large role in subsiding the feeling of not being able to catch up.

The first transformation is grace. Rather than being hypercritical of every little detail in our lives, we will assess ourselves as a whole. This is like receiving a score on a test based off all questions rather than one. This comprehensive view dilutes the magnitude of each small mistake that feels like a big deal. The second transformation is awareness. We will be aware of the choices we have available each day and how their outcomes may affect our lives. The third transformation is momentum. Once we have clarity in our choices, we may continue making decisions that lead to our version of holistic success.

For example, a professional may be faced with the choice of spending extra time preparing for a presentation or leaving the office early to make dinner with their family. It will be up to them to make the decision that lends the largest amount of happiness to their life. However, by reviewing themselves holistically, this professional will be able to accept the outcome of either decision as well as see how the decision may potentially impact them later on. Once they have made the choice, they are on their way to gaining momentum. They no longer separate work and life but integrate the two to their benefit.

The fourth transformation is empowerment. Through a holistic view of ourselves, we are free to be imperfect and make choices that lead us to the next positive step. We will be able to continue to make choices that make us happy—no longer trying to juggle things separately that should work together.

Jay Shetty—author, former monk, and business coach—has similar thoughts on the concept of balance. While discussing this topic in 2019, a friend complained to Shetty that finding balance for himself is incredibly difficult. His friend explained that he loves his business. His business is his purpose and what makes him happy, but when he is in a relationship, falling in love consumes him. His partner becomes his top priority and work falls to the wayside. He asked Shetty, "My business is what drives me, it's what my passion is, what excites me, it's what I love doing every single day. How do I fit a relationship [into that]?"

Shetty responded to his friend, "I think the challenge is just the perception that we have to fit stuff in." That language automatically separates different aspects of our lives, when in reality both work and a relationship has positive and negative effects on our body, mind, and consciousness. They are interconnected. Rather than think of every aspect of our lives like puzzle pieces, they should be thought of like threads woven together in a tapestry, each thread enhancing the strength and beauty of the next.

This tapestry mindset is how we begin to see the different areas of our lives supporting each other. When one "thread" is not strong enough, we can see the others holding it in place. In this view, the question of finding a partner goes from, "What gap do they fill in my life?" to, "How are we enhancing each other to be better?" (How do I Find Balance in My Life?, 2018) Everything should not necessarily fit together like a puzzle, but be integrated together like a tapestry.

We often think of our lives like a puzzle where each aspect has to "fit" perfectly in its place to gain clarity. This is not the case. Whether you need to view it as achieving worklife balance or worklife integration, it is something that must be sought after in the Holistic Dream.

OFF BALANCE, ON PURPOSE

Picture a gymnast. They have just run, done some sort of impressive series of flips, and launched themselves onto a balance beam in a handstand position. Their palms serve as the base holding their weight up on a thin piece of board. The gymnast has achieved perfect balance.

If you look closer, you will notice that there is truly no such thing as perfect balance when gravity has something to say about it. The gymnast, even while exhibiting perfect form, must make microadjustments to keep from falling. This is exactly how balancing work and life goes. Even when you feel like you have achieved it perfectly, you are still making microadjustments to keep everything from collapsing in on itself. And, just like the gymnast, we hold ourselves to a ridiculously high expectation of perfect balance. This can be exhausting.

The good news is we can follow a new philosophy that does not stifle our happiness based on unreasonable measures. According to Dan Thurmon—president of Motivation Works, Inc.—this philosophy is living "Off balance, on purpose." (2013)

One way to look at balance is as settling for the status quo or maintaining. Picture the gymnast again. In their handstand position, they are working very hard to keep their balance, but their hard work does not change their performance. If they do it right, the image the audience sees stays the same. Eventually, even while defying gravity, the gymnast enters their comfort zone and the handstand becomes easy. This is how life balance can be. We begin to go through the motions and live off "muscle memory." This puts us directly in our comfort zone, and in our comfort zone there is no growth.

Being off balance means living outside of our normal patterns and this is where transformation and change happen. Being off balance is our reality. As Thurmon states, "You have to be off balance in order to learn, grow, love, serve others, or improve yourself in any meaningful way." We must embrace the uncertainty.

It is true that some of my most off-balance times are when I have experienced the most growth. Shortly after college graduation, I was broke, working three jobs, and just generally not loving life. My free time was extremely limited, and I was barely making ends meet. This was not the outcome I was expecting after working so hard for my degree, and I was disappointed in myself and my schooling.

Something I had always struggled with is patience, and this time in my life really tested it. After about a year, I had probably done close to fifteen first round interviews on top of countless applications that never garnered a response at all. I had gotten so close on a few occasions, getting to second and third round interviews, but never made the final cut. I was discussing all of this with one of my mentors, who was actually executive director of the nonprofit where I worked at the time. We worked together for a few years, and she became my confidant and sometimes unofficial life coach. The advice she gave me was to, "Just chill." I was trying too hard and putting too much pressure on myself.

I knew my worth. I knew that anywhere I went I would be a good employee, fast learner, and add value in some manner. The fact I could not seem to demonstrate this to hiring managers absolutely destroyed me. To my mentor, all this mental anguish was entirely unnecessary, because as simple as it sounds, the right position would come along. I just had to be patient.

I stopped filling out applications for about two months and just did nothing. This is entirely offbrand for me. When there is something that I know I can be doing to improve my day-today life, I try to do it. However, sitting still in my discomfort was the best thing for me and my patience developed exponentially. I noticed this not only internally but also in how I interacted with other people. While patience will be a lifelong journey for me, I am thankful for this offbalance time in my life to help make it a little stronger.

And sure enough, my mentor was right—I was recruited for the position I am in now, and I love it. By allowing myself to be off balance for a time, I not only experienced personal growth but also got the outcome I was looking for. Sometimes being off balance on purpose will be necessary for holistic success.

IT'S UP TO US

"I found it quite easy to balance work and life when I didn't have any work," said Nigel Marsh—Australian underwater photojournalist, author, and marketer—in his 2010 TED talk "How to Make WorkLife Balance Work." Marsh had made it part of his purpose to figure out what works in achieving balance. He spent the last several years studying and writing about this topic and has found that achieving balance is each individual's personal responsibility.

According to Marsh, governments and corporations are not going to solve the issue of worklife balance for us. In the United States, we have seen the implementation of certain perks and services meant to make achieving worklife balance easier. These include casual Fridays, paternity leave, onsite childcare, and the list goes on. However, as Marsh stated, "There are thousands and thousands of people out there living lives in quiet, screaming desperation, where they work long, hard hours at jobs they hate, to enable them to buy things they don't need to impress people they don't like." People are not happy, and they are taught to prioritize "things" only making them more miserable. Simply adding casual Fridays is not really getting down to the core of the issue.

Leaving lifestyle balance in the hands of someone else means we are probably not going to like it. Work costs employers money, which makes employees an expensive resource. It is in employer's nature, and best interest, to squeeze every productivity dollar possible out of each employee. This is true of even the most well-intentioned companies. If in the position to, we have to be responsible for setting and maintaining the boundaries we want to have in our lives.

With balance we need to be realistic. We often try to judge our lifestyle off a singular day, and most often the bad ones. As Marsh stated, "We can do it all, just not in one day." We need to elongate our concept of balance over time and understand that it will ebb and flow as life does. According to Marsh the trick is not getting trapped into the mindset of "I'll have a life when I retire." This attitude makes every responsibility feel like an obligation or chore and causes us to miss out on daily life.

Even if not focused on retirement yet, many of us are waiting for "the next big thing" to happen until we will officially start living. Waiting until a college acceptance, higher paying job, larger house, dedicated partner, or so on comes along to feel like balance has been achieved or is achievable thwarts happiness. Our version of balance must be a daily, intentional practice, even when life demands otherwise.

Marsh told the story of a friend who had visited him and said, "Nigel, I have read your book and recognized that my life is completely out of balance." She was inundated with work, in the office for ten hours a day, and commuting for two hours. She no longer had any personal relationships, only work relationships. She stated, "I have decided to get a grip and sort it out, I've joined a gym!"

Marsh paused. Then he responded, "Being a fit tenhour a day office rat isn't more balanced, it's more fit." There is a lot more to life than that—there is also the intellectual, emotional, and spiritual side. To be truly balanced, you have to attend to all areas.

This can be daunting. As Marsh put it, "I can't get fit, you want me to go to church and call my mother too?" That is the issue, right? There is a lot we have to do and a lot we would like to do, and it is our responsibility to make it fit. But how is that humanly possible? This query reminded Marsh of another story.

A few years back, his wife called and asked him to pick up their son Harry from school because she had somewhere to be that evening with their other children. Marsh left work an hour early, picked Harry up, and walked to a nearby park. They played some games and split a pizza at a café. After, they went home and had bath time. Soon it was time for bed and Marsh outfitted Harry in his Batman pajamas and read him a chapter of *James and the Giant Peach*.

As Marsh was walking out of Harry's bedroom after kissing him goodnight, Harry exclaimed, "Dad, this has been the best day of my life ever!" (Ibid.)

Marsh and his son had not spent the day at Disney World. Marsh had not really done anything exceptional for Harry that day. But, according to Marsh, "The small things matter." Finding balance does not mean an entire overhaul in your daytoday activities or creating dramatic shifts in your habits. "It's the smallest investments in the right places." This is how you can radically improve the quality of your life and relationships.

CONCLUSION

Living in holistic success means living in your version of balance—not sacrificing personal success in mind, body, soul, or business for greater success in one domain. Balance, and the kind of balance that feels doable to us, ebbs and flows throughout life. Whether it is living traditionally balanced, integrated, or off balance on purpose, the important truth here is taking responsibility for finding a version of balance that works for you.

As Nigel Marsh said perfectly, it is time we change our definition of success away from "The person with the most money when he dies wins, to a more thoughtful and balanced definition of what a life welllived looks like." (Ibid.) It is up to us to adopt different measures of success for ourselves and society. In holistic success, we will prioritize all areas of our lives and find individualized balance.

DISCUSSION QUESTIONS
1. What version of balance would work best for you in this moment in time: traditional balance, integration, or off balance, on purpose?
2. Have you ever experienced growth during an offbalanced time in your life?
3. What small ways can you start investing in the areas of your life that are "off" to bring yourself back to equilibrium?

KEY TAKEAWAYS

1. There is not one kind of balance, and finding the one that works for you is essential.
2. We need to make the areas of our lives work together, not necessarily "fit" together.
3. Being off balance can be a starting point for personal growth.

PART THREE

WHERE ARE WE GOING?

CONCLUSION: THE FUTURE IS BRIGHT!

Big houses, fancy cars, high salaries, social ranking—this is what the picture of success has become in the United States. We are fed a pathway to success throughout childhood in the form of the broken American Dream. While very little US political doctrine is founded in equality, the American Dream is meant for all. And this is one of the largest lies we are told by our culture.

While there are stories of individuals literally "picking themselves up by their bootstraps," working hard, and actually achieving the American Dream, most of us are impeded by unassailable barriers to entry in American society. Having Black or Brown skin, being a woman, identifying as LGBTQ+, or living in the wrong geographic area make achieving the American Dream harder. Often an intersection of even just two of the previously listed items make it impossible. I can predict some individuals may argue "that's life—no one claimed the American Dream is easy." I counter that a national ethos which is exclusionary to most of the population is an injustice.

Additionally, many tenets of the American Dream have to do with attaining wealth. Wanting financial security is not a bad thing and is often necessary for survival. However, wealth has become a main focal point of success. The economics of our country make it so wealth cannot be accessed by all, making 99 percent of us feel like failures. It does not have to be this way.

It is time we redefine success for ourselves; we need holistic success. There is a lot more that makes life great than what the American Dream considers. What is more, often the pursuit of the American Dream distracts us from all the good around us. Our new definition of success must prioritize human connection, passion, innovation, balance, and future thinking. Through these priorities we will find personalized success in mind, body, soul, and business.

The first steps to achieving holistic success are personal, individual, internal changes. Making internal adjustments or mindset shifts may not be easy, but the results will be worth it. Through redefining success for ourselves we will renew our purpose, create intentional life plans, and enjoy our daytoday experiences.

Then we tackle social change. Social change begins when enough people believe there is a better way of living and start following it. If enough individuals adopt the concept of holistic success in their personal lives, we will see a community strengthened through a common purpose, increased collaboration among social groups, and innovation to solve some of our most pressing problems.

Implementing holistic success means we have a lot to look forward to! Not only will we be happier as individuals but also the changes we implement will be for the betterment of future society.

WE HAVE TO ADJUST INTERNALLY FIRST ...
Our internal changes must be focused on personal happiness. We do this by going unapologetically all in on our passions, forging connections to build strong personal relationships, and investing in our free time or activities seen as unproductive, like playtime.

Step 1) *Go "All In" on Your Passion and Define Success for Yourself*
Forget about the American Dream, societal expectations, and what you have learned about what success looks like. Now think about what makes you get out of bed every day; think about what makes you happy. Some will need to stick to the high salary and status definition of success, for some the tiny house craze might be calling their name, and others may want to spend as many minutes as possible of the day with their children. In reality, most of our definitions are a combination of things that fall into the categories of mind, body, soul, and business.

We must define success for ourselves. Each individual aiming towards one definition of success centered on wealth, is self-damaging. As people, we have a tendency to stake our entire future happiness on the success of our finances. We also place a lot of our and others' value on societal status and wealth. Too many of us feel like failures because of this. Through holistic success, we will evaluate ourselves as a whole, rather than by one part of our total sum. We will do this holistic evaluation while only answering to our personal definition of success.

Finally, for this first step—accept your new definition of success and drop the previous expectations you had created.

Step 2) *Become a Human Connection Guru*
Dr. Starla Fitch told the story of a surgical tech, named Joe, she had the pleasure of working with on a number of occasions. (2015) The facility they both worked for was facing cutbacks; hours were cut, perks even as low as the staff coffee pot were removed, and everyone was on the verge of burnout. Morale was at an alltime low and the negative energy was palpable throughout the office. Because of this, Dr. Fitch decided to implement a daily morning gratitude practice. The practice became quite the hit and soon everyone wanted to share their threeitem gratitude list with Dr. Fitch.

One day when Joe was assigned to be Dr. Fitch's surgical tech, he shook his head when asked for his gratitude list. Joe just could not come up with three items he was thankful for. Joe was normally a willing participant and was clearly having a tough day. In response, Dr. Fitch asked everyone in the room to share three things about Joe they were grateful for. Through this exercise, everyone learned that Joe is an individual that truly goes above and beyond. He is the one that comes in early to warm the blankets for patients, and he is also the one that stays late getting the rooms ready for the next day. Everyone felt connected to Joe and Joe felt seen. Joe was almost moved to tears—it only took that small amount of human connection to make his lousy workday better. Human connection is vital for happiness.

Shame, including shame from not achieving the American Dream, undermines the vulnerability that enables us to connect with each other. We have to overcome our shame with a tolerance for imperfection, selfforgiveness, and by not allowing others to evaluate our lives. Overcoming shame is required to build meaningful human connection.

Step 3) *Make Time to Play*
To achieve holistic success, we have to make time to play!

Paul Dixon—a professional with over a decade's worth of experience in the toy industry with Disney and Target—opened a talk he gave with the question, "What was your favorite toy as a child?" (2018) He explained that his was an NFL electric football set, which was essentially a mini version of a football field with players that buzz around the field playing the game. With Dixon's experience, he recounted a time he got an idea: "What if I actually bought my favorite [childhood] toy and played with this toy for thirty consecutive days?"

Dixon pondered this question for some time and then finally decided to do it. He bought the electric football set. After his first day playing with the toy, he recalled thinking, "Wow, that was just a fun experience!"

Dixon played with the NFL electric football set for thirty days and had a few memories along the way. In the first, having grown up in Minneapolis, Minnesota, he remembered how much he used to love cheering on the Minnesota Vikings. He also remembered how much fun he would have—as an introverted and shy kid—escaping into this game. Then he wondered, "As adults, are we actually having enough fun, are we allowing ourselves to be a child again?" Dixon explained that in the hustle and bustle of our daily lives it often seems very challenging to take time to do something for ourselves, to just have fun.

We are trained that play is purposeless, and with play often comes guilt. Individuals tend to feel like they are shirking their responsibilities and letting down those around them when not fully focused on personal obligations. We have it all wrong. Play has the ability to increase productivity, learning, and job satisfaction, as well as reduce stress and help us connect with others. In the holistic success we must prioritize play.

With holistic success we will have more balance, passion, and people doing what they love every day with intentionally designed goals.

... THEN WE CAN WORK TO ADJUST OUR EXTERNAL ENVIRONMENTS

If we begin with enough individuals making the internal changes of redefining success, finding passion, practicing vulnerability, creating connection, and finding time to play, we will soon be able to reflect these changes for the betterment of society.

There was a recent study done at University of Pennsylvania and published in *Science Magazine* that investigated the tipping point required for the minority of a sufficiently large group to change the social norm. The researchers found that it only takes 25 percent of a group to enact change. (Centola et al. 2018) Twenty-five percent! It is my belief that if enough people can adopt the internal changes required for holistic success, those changes will soon be reflected outward in society.

As a result of increased human connection in personal holistic success, we will soon see increased collaboration.

Step 4) *Collaborate*
Dr. Shelle VanEtten de Sánchez—director of Cultural Services for the city of Albuquerque, New Mexico—is absolutely committed to collaboration. Sanchez's love for collaboration comes from a place of scarcity: "I came to this place from not enough, from not enough resources, not enough money, not enough time to achieve the work that could be done, and sometimes, even the work that should be done." (2014) But she realized that the right partners and collaborators can make all the difference.

Sánchez's favorite example of collaboration was a poetry meets performance exercise imagined by poet Valerie Marina. Poetry is not known for being a collaborative art form, rather it tends to be intensely personal. Knowing this, Marina had a group of poets work for weeks creating finished, polished, beautiful poems. Then they all met together and took turns reading their work for the group. Once everyone had their opportunity to present their poem, each person passed their poem one individual over. The individual now in possession of their poem had complete agency to cut it up into words, sentences, and verses as they saw fit.

All the poem fragments were placed in the middle of a table and then as a group they reassembled the individual work into one collaborative piece. The collaboration was beautiful, and the ownership was shared among all poets in attendance. As Sánchez put it, "You never know what will happen when you release an idea to a group or pass a poem to somebody else, but with the right partners it leads to bigger and better things." There is power in diverse individuals with diverse resources working towards the same goal—this is the birthplace for innovation. Collaboration really is where the magic happens because that is where innovation lives.

Step 5) *Innovate*
Halfway through his experiment in 1928, Sir Alexander Fleming—Scottish physician and microbiologist—up and left for a twoweek vacation. Fleming left a petri dish with a bacteria culture in the lab sink while he was gone. His petri dish had become mistakenly contaminated with a mold. Fleming noticed that the mold had prevented the bacteria from growing and had even started killing bacteria cells. This was the official discovery of the first naturally occurring antibiotic—penicillin. (Kulvaitis, 2008)

Fleming's unintentional innovation brought us the most widely used antibiotic in the world. Fleming stated, "One sometimes finds what one is not looking for. When I woke up just after dawn on Sept. 28, 1928, I certainly didn't plan to revolutionize all medicine by discovering the world's first antibiotic, or bacteria killer. But I guess that was exactly what I did." (Fleming, 1929) Imagine the problems we could solve if we actually put our minds to it. Innovation is where problems are solved and is required for a brighter future.

With holistic success we will have greater sense of unity, increased collaboration, and groundbreaking innovation.

LET'S TAKE ACTION

Society may be a mess currently, but if we can follow our new dream of holistic success, our future looks bright! We will create a future that every individual can benefit from when it comes to personal success. This change will start within each of us.

We must work towards individualized, holistic success in mind, body, soul, and business. Then we have to prioritize human connection, playtime, and balance.

Once we have adjusted internally, society will become a more collaborative place where our most important problems are solved and future generations benefit. Through these changes, I see a community less divided due to a common, achievable goal. This goal will no longer be the pursuit of the American Dream, but rather for a better individual reflection of what a life well lived looks like.

I cannot wait for you to join me on the journey to our new dream: holistic success!

ACKNOWLEDGMENTS

SPECIAL RECOGNITION
Thank you to Cooper Prindl, Rachel Mazzara, and Tommy Borin for helping bring my book to life!

A big shoutout to Jacob Conant for always believing in me!

A Big Thank You to the Following Individuals for Their Endless Support:

Megan Brown
Eric Koester
Keara Clacko
Jacob Conant
Thomas Borin
Kelly Ray
Maddy Rockhold
Rachel Mazzara
Molly Rockwood
Katie Zacharias
Chad Pawlak Jr.

Maria Corbin
Jake Breit
Abigail Fox
Anthony Hunt
Morgan Milas
Julie Benzschawel
Lisa Attonito
Myles Brown Hunt
Marcus Taylor
Easton McChesney
Ryan Stock

Meghan Ryan
Karley Kryzanski
Connor Curran
Madison Wicks
Bennett Whittemore
Trevor Suarez
Gina Pagan
Connor McColl
Adria Shelley
Lori Ogle
Jackie Labonite
Mitch Brown
Joyann McChesney
Michele Pogodzinski
Kristi Miller
Matthew Ramos
Mariah Vojtasek
Brooke Card
Paul Butrico
Daniel Donchev
Kelsey Brodt
Christiaan Nel
Cooper Prindl
Joanna Rivas
Deb DuLyn

Zak Van Voorhees
Nicole deGuzman
Petrina Zaraszczak
Maureen Borin
Craig Simpkins
Katarina Petranovich
Gregory Stromberg
JoLanda Rogers
Monica S. ShahDavidson
Lindsey Rykal
Lisa Attonito
Kimberly Heinzelman
Robert Holtz
Jared Phillips
Robin Fosterling
Lauren Brayden
Ali TahlerReed
Janalee Knapmiller
Thomas M. Van Cleave
Heather Barwick
Jared Phillips
Alissa Pescheck
Kathleen McGillis
Dionne Grayson

APPENDIX

INTRODUCTION

Carter, Shawn. "Less than 20% of Americans Say They're Living the American Dream - Here's Why." *CNBC*, September 19, 2017. https://www.cnbc.com/2017/09/19/less-than-20-percent-of-americans-say-theyre-living-the-american-dream.html

Chiwaya, Nigel and Janell Ross. "The American Dream While Black: Locked in a Vicious Cycle." *NBC News*, August 3, 2020. https://www.nbcnews.com/specials/american-dream-while-black-homeownership/

Diamond, Anna. "The Original Meanings of the "American Dream" and "America First" Were Starkly Different From How We Use Them Today." *Smithsonian Magazine*, October 2018. https://www.smithsonianmag.com/history/behold-america-american-dream-slogan-book-sarah-churchwell-180970311/

Encyclopaedia Britannica Online. s.v. "Culture and Society in the Great Depression." Accessed June 12, 2021. https://www.

britannica.com/event/Great-Depression/Economic-impact#ref234457

Flynn, Andrea, Dorian Warren, Felicia Wong, and Susan Holmberg. *Rewrite the Racial Rules: Building an Inclusive American Economy*. Boston: Roosevelt Institute, 2016. https://rooseveltinstitute.org/wp-content/uploads/2016/06/RI-RRT-Race-201606.pdf

Fullwood III, Sam. "Continuing Inequalities Blur the American Dream." *Center for American Progress*, June 23, 2016. https://www.americanprogress.org/issues/race/news/2016/06/23/140313/continuing-inequalities-blur-the-american-dream/

Kelly, Jack. "Billionaires Are Getting Richer During The COVID-19 Pandemic While Most Americans Suffer." *Forbes*, April 27, 2020. https://www.forbes.com/sites/jackkelly/2020/04/27/billionaires-are-getting-richer-during-the-covid-19-pandemic-while-most-americans-suffer/?sh=46906c44804f

Schwantes, Marcel. "Science Says 92 Percent of People Don't Achieve Their Goals. Here's How the Other 8 Percent Do." *Inc.*, June 26, 2016. https://www.inc.com/marcel-schwantes/science-says-92-percent-of-people-dont-achieve-goals-heres-how-the-other-8-perce.html

WelfareInfo. "Poverty in Compton, California." Last Modified 2017. https://www.welfareinfo.org/poverty-rate/california/compton

CHAPTER 1

Brooks, Arthur C. "'Success Addicts' Choose Being Special Over Being Happy." *The Atlantic*, July 30, 2020. https://www.theatlantic.com/family/archive/2020/07/why-success-wont-make-you-happy/614731/

Cancialoci, Chris. "4 Reasons Social Capital Trumps All." *Forbes*, September 22, 2014. https://www.forbes.com/sites/chriscancialosi/2014/09/22/4-reasons-social-capital-trumps-all/?sh=2b-3ca37e6986

Centers for Disease Control and Prevention. "Common Barriers to Participation Experienced by People with Disabilities." Disability and Health Promotion. Accessed June 24, 2021. https://www.cdc.gov/ncbddd/disabilityandhealth/disability-barriers.html

Eustachewich, Lia. "Felicity Huffman, Lori Loughlin Busted in College Admissions Cheating Scandal." *New York Post*, March 12, 2019. https://nypost.com/2019/03/12/lori-loughlin-felicity-huffman-busted-in-college-admissions-cheating-scandal/

Joiner, Thomas. Lonely at the Top. New York: St. Martin's Press, 2011. 134.

Northeastern University College of Professional Studies. "Fall 2012 Graduation Speaker, Dennis Lehane, Encourages Graduates to be Unafraid to Fail." Northeastern University. press release, October 18, 2012. Northeastern University. website. https://cps.northeastern.edu/news/fall-2012-graduation-speaker-dennis-lehane-encourages-graduates-be-unafraid-fail/

Northwestern Mutual. "1 In 3 Americans Have Less Than $5,000 In Retirement Savings." Northwestern Mutual. press release, May 8, 2018. Northwestern Mutual. website. https://news.northwesternmutual.com/2018-05-08-1-In-3-Americans-Have-Less-Than-5-000-In-Retirement-Savings

O'Connor, Cailin, Carrie Finkbiner, and Linda Watson. *Adverse Childhood Experiences in Wisconsin: Findings from the 2010 Behavioral Risk Factor Survey.* Madison, WI: Wisconsin Children's Trust Fund and Child Abuse Prevention Fund of Children's Hospital & Health System, 2012. https://media.wcwpds.wisc.edu/preservice/human_behavior/docs/WisconsinACEs.pdf

Perez, Zenen Jaimes. "Left Behind: How LGBT Young People are Excluded from Economic Prosperity." *Center for American Progress*, July 16, 2014. https://www.americanprogress.org/issues/lgbtq rights/reports/2014/07/16/93901/left-behind/

The Pew Charitable Trusts. *Pursuing the American Dream: Economic Mobility in America.* Washington, D.C.: ThePew Charitable Trusts, 2012. https://www.pewtrusts.org/~/media/legacy/uploadedfiles/pcs_assets/2012/pursuingamericandreampdf.pdf

Soergal, Andrew. "4 States Control 80 Percent of Venture Capitalist Dollars." *U.S. News*, May 19, 2018. https://www.usnews.com/news/best-states/articles/2018-05-10/4-states-control-80-percent-of-venture-capital-dollars

University of Minnesota Libraries. "2.4 The Consequences of Poverty." Social Problems. Accessed June 24, 2021. https://open.

lib.umn.edu/socialproblems/chapter/2-4-the-consequences-of-poverty/

Vance, J.D. "America's Forgotten Working Class." Filmed September 2016 in New York, NY. TEDNYC video, 14:33. https://www.ted.com/talks/j_d_vance_america_s_forgotten_working_class

Ward, Deborah E., Lora E. Park, Kristin Naragon-Gainey. "Can't Buy Me Love (or Friendship): Social Consequences of Financially Contingent Self-Worth." *Personality and Social Bulletin* 46, no. 12 (March 19, 2020): 1665-16691. https://doi.org/10.1177/0146167220910872

CHAPTER 2

Adkins, Amy. "Millennials: The Job-Hopping Generation." *Gallup Business Journal*, Accessed June 12, 2021. https://www.gallup.com/workplace/231587/millennials-job-hopping-generation.aspx

Botton, Alain de. "A Kinder, Gentler Philosophy of Success." Filmed July 2009 in Oxford, England. TED video, 16:14. https://www.ted.com/talks/alain_de_botton_a_kinder_gentler_philosophy_of_success#t-1102

Brooks, David. "The Lies Our Culture Tells Us About What Matters - And a Better Way to Live." Filmed April 2019 in Vancouver, BC. TED video, 14.44. https://www.ted.com/talks/david_brooks_the_lies_our_culture_tells_us_about_what_matters_and_a_better_way_to_live#t-849448

Hall, John. "The Trend Toward a New Definition of Success and Why it's Important to You." *Forbes*, September 9, 2018. https://www.forbes.com/sites/johnhall/2018/09/09/the-trend-toward-a-new-definition-of-success-and-why-its-important-to-you/?sh=2021df47e45c

Martin, Courtney. "The New American Dream." Filmed February 2016 in Vancouver, BC. TED video, 14.23. https://www.ted.com/talks/courtney_e_martin_the_new_american_dream

Pew Research Center. "How the Great Recession Has Changed Life in America." Retirement. Accessed June 30, 2010. https://www.pewresearch.org/social-trends/2010/06/30/how-the-great-recession-has-changed-life-in-america/

CHAPTER 3

Barth, F. Diane. "Does Talk Therapy Really Work? One Researcher Looks at the Data." *The Couch (blog)*. *Psychology Today*, November 6, 2010. psychologytoday.com/us/blog/the-couch/201011/does-talk-therapy-really-work

Brown, Brene. "The Power of Vulnerability." Filmed June 2010 in Houston, TX. TEDxHouston video, 20:03. https://www.ted.com/talks/brene_brown_the_power_of_vulnerability?language=en

Kammerer, Annette. "The Scientific Underpinnings and Impacts of Shame." *Scientific American*, August 9, 2019. https://www.scientificamerican.com/article/the-scientific-underpinnings-and-impacts-of-shame/

Policarpio, Nicole. "'The One Advice That Made Kevin Hart Famous." *Nicole Policarpio (blog)*. *Medium*, February 7, 2018. https://medium.com/@nicopolicarpio/the-one-advice-that-made-kevin-hart-famous-39702855b9e7

Simon, Katharina A., Georg A. Hollander, and Andrew McMichael. "Evolution of the Immune System in Humans from Infancy to Old Age." *Proceedings: Biological Sciences* 282, no. 1821 (December 22, 2015): 1-3. https://doi.org/10.1098/rspb.2014.3085

Wete, Brad. "Kevin Hart on how 'Laugh at My Pain' got a Top 10 Box Office Debut." *Entertainment Weekly*, September 13, 2011. https://ew.com/article/2011/09/13/kevin-hart-laugh-at-my-pain-top-10-box-office/

Wolpert, Stuart. "UCLA Neuroscientist's Book Explains Why Social Connection is as Important as Food and Shelter." *UCLA Newsroom*, October 10, 2013. https://newsroom.ucla.edu/releases/we-are-hard-wired-to-be-social-248746

CHAPTER 4

Alikhani, Amir. "Is American Individualism Hurting Our Teams at Work?" *Hackernoon (blog)*. *Medium*, July 1, 2019. https://medium.com/hackernoon/is-american-individualism-hurting-our-teams-at-work-cdad9c591577

Andre, Claire and Manuel Velasquez. "Creating the Good Society." Santa Clarita University Ethics. Accessed June 14, 2021. https://www.scu.edu/mcae/publications/iie/v5n1.1.html

Boscari, Stafenia, Thomas Bartolotti, Torbjorn H. Netland, and Nick Rich. "National Culture and Operations Management: A Structured Literature Review." *International Journal of Production Research* 56, no. 18 (April 24, 2018): 6314-6331. https://doi.org/10.1080/00207543.2018.1461275

Huddleston Jr., Tom. "Tony Robbins: Money Doesn't Equal Happiness — Here's What Does." *CNBC Make It*, March 28, 2019. https://www.cnbc.com/2019/03/28/tony-robbins-money-isnt-the-source-of-lasting-happiness.html

Jones, Benjamin F. "The Science Behind the Growing Importance of Collaboration." *Kellogg Insight*, September 6, 2017. https://insight.kellogg.northwestern.edu/article/the-science-behind-the-growing-importance-of-collaboration

Partners Healthcare. "Individualism." U.S. and American Culture. Accessed July 14, 2021. https://pips.partners.org/life-in-the-united-states/american-culture/individualism.aspx

Shirky, Clay. "Institutions vs. Collaboration." Filmed July 2005 in Oxford, England. TEDGlobal video, 20:35. https://www.ted.com/talks/clay_shirky_institutions_vs_collaboration#t-200596

Tapscott, Don. "Four Principles for the Open World." Filmed June 2012 in Edinburgh, Scotland. TEDGlobal video, 17:33. https://www.ted.com/talks/don_tapscott_four_principles_for_the_open_world?language=en

Tufekci, Zeynap. "Social Media's Small, Positive Role in Human Relationships." *The Atlantic*, April 25, 2012. https://www.

theatlantic.com/technology/archive/2012/04/social-medias-small-positive-role-in-human-relationships/256346/

Wilhelmsen, Tabitha Russell. "How to Create a Culture of Collaboration in the Workplace." *Great Place to Work (blog)*. *Great Place to Work*, May 2nd, 2019. https://www.greatplacetowork.com/resources/blog/how-to-create-a-culture-of-collaboration-in-the-workplace

CHAPTER 5

Barnett, Lynn A. "Developmental Benefits of Play for Children." *Journal of Leisure Research* 22, no. 2 (April 1990): 138-153. https://doi.org/10.1080/00222216.1990.11969821

Brown, Stuart. "Play is More Than Just Fun." Filmed May 2008 in Pasadena, CA. TED video, 26:21. https://www.ted.com/talks/stuart_brown_play_is_more_than_just_fun?language=en#t-1237178

Chillag, Amy. "Why Adults Should Play, Too." *CNN Health*, November 2, 2017. https://www.cnn.com/2017/11/02/health/why-adults-should-play-too/index.html

Davis, Matt. "Why More Play is the Key to Creativity and Productivity." *Big Think*, October 24, 2019. https://bigthink.com/personal-growth/play-creativity?rebelltitem=1#rebelltitem1

Julson, Erica. "10 Best Ways to Increase Dopamine Levels Naturally." *Healthline*, May 10, 2018. https://www.healthline.com/nutrition/how-to-increase-dopamine

Sprankles, Julie. "David Beckham Just Stayed Up Until 3AM Building a Lego Hogwarts Castle for His Daughter, Harper." *Yahoo Entertainment*, September 8, 2019. https://www.yahoo.com/entertainment/david-beckham-just-stayed-until-021004410.html

Tartakovsky, Margarita. "The Importance of Play for Adults." *PsychCentral (blog)*. November 15, 2012. https://psychcentral.com/blog/the-importance-of-play-for-adults#1

The Tonight Show Starring Jimmy Fallon. "David Beckham Reacts to Wife Victoria Trolling Him on Instagram for His Lego Obsession." Video, 5:30. February 27, 2020. https://www.youtube.com/watch?v=_aFUnBErsts

CHAPTER 6

Abolfathi, Niloofar and Simone Santamaria. "Dating Disruption - How Tinder Gamified an Industry." *MIT Sloan Management Review*, February 13, 2020. https://sloanreview.mit.edu/article/dating-disruption-how-tinder-gamified-an-industry/

Dasgupta, Ipsita. "To Challenge the Status Quo, Find a Co-Conspirator." Filmed September 2019 in Mumbai, India. TED@BCGMumbai video, 10:54. https://www.ted.com/talks/ipsita_dasgupta_to_challenge_the_status_quo_find_a_co_conspirator?language=en

Levi, Primo. *The Periodic Table*. New York: Shocken Books, 1984. 150-159.

Raz, Guy. "Bumble: Whitney Wolf." October 16, 2017. In *How I Built This*. Produced by NPR. Podcast, MP3 audio, 42:50. https://www.npr.org/2017/11/29/557437086/bumble-whitney-wolfe

Wozniak, Steve. "How Do You Dream Bigger." Interview by Eric Koester. *Creator Institute*, June 23, 2021.

CHAPTER 7

Ferriss, Tim. "Fear-Setting: The Most Valuable Exercise I Do Every Month." *The Tim Ferriss Show* (blog). May 15th, 2017. https://tim.blog/2017/05/15/fear-setting/

Gilbert, Elizabeth. "Success, Failure and the Drive to Keep Creating." filmed March 2014 in Vancouver, BC. TED video, 7:05. https://www.ted.com/talks/elizabeth_gilbert_success_failure_and_the_drive_to_keep_creating#t-335784

Holiday, Ryan. "The Surprising Value of Negative Thinking." *The Obstacle is the Way* (blog). *Psychology Today*, May 1, 2014. https://www.psychologytoday.com/us/blog/the-obstacle-is-the-way/201405/the-surprising-value-negative-thinking

In Depth with Graham Bensinger. "Rob Dyrdek: I Made $17 on my $1.8 Million Movie." March 10, 2016. Video, 3:49. https://www.youtube.com/watch?v=6oTLC5uSPyo

Keller, Gary. *The One Thing: The Surprising Truth Behind Extraordinary Results*. Austin: Bard Press, 2012. 45-52.

Kelly, Jack. "More Than Half of U.S. Workers Are Unhappy In Their Jobs: Here's Why And What Needs To Be Done Now."

Forbes, October 25, 2019. https://www.forbes.com/sites/jackkelly/2019/10/25/more-than-half-of-us-workers-are-unhappy-in-their-jobs-heres-why-and-what-needs-to-be-done-now/?sh=1fe752f52024

Rothwell, Jonathan and Steve Crabtree. *Not Just a Job: New Evidence on the Quality of Work in the United States*. Washington D.C.: Gallup, 2019. https://www.luminafoundation.org/wp-content/uploads/2019/11/not-just-a-job-new-evidence-on-the-quality-of-work-in-the-united-states.pdf

Russell, Joel. "Staying on a Roll: Skateboarder Rob Dyrdek relies on licensing deals to maintain revenue as age dims his sporting skills." *Los Angeles Business Journal*, May 24, 2010. https://labusinessjournal.com/news/2010/may/24/staying-roll/

Shetty, Jay. "Rob Dyrdek: Dropping out of School and Becoming and Entrepreneur." April 9, 2019. In *On Purpose with Jay Shetty*. Produced by Jay Shetty. Podcast, MPS audio, 84:07. https://jayshetty.me/podcast/rob-dyrdek/

Skipper, Clay. "Why You Should Design a Life—and Workout Plan—That Makes You Uncomfortable." *GQ*, January 13, 2019. https://www.gq.com/story/ido-portal-make-yourself-uncomfortable

CHAPTER 8

Anders, Charlie Jane. "Go Ahead, Dream About the Future." Filmed December 2019 in New York, NY. TEDWomen video, 10:38. https://www.ted.com/talks/charlie_jane_anders_go_ahead_dream_about_the_future#t-65177

Bill and Melinda Gates Foundation. "Our Work: Water, Sanitation & Hygiene." Accessed June 8th, 2021. https://www.gatesfoundation.org/our-work/programs/global-growth-and-opportunity/water-sanitation-and-hygiene

Fitzpatrick, Alex. "Why the U.S. is Losing the War on COVID-19." *Time*, March 30, 2020. https://time.com/5879086/us-covid-19/

TEDx Talks. "Prof. Dr. J. Rod Franklin: Thinking Differently for a Better Future." April 19, 2016. Video, 20:24. https://www.youtube.com/watch?v=o5RdSIWwoog

Wallach, Ari. "3 Ways to Plan for the (Very) Long Term." Filmed October 2016 in Washington, DC. TEDxMidAtlantic video, 13:34. https://www.ted.com/talks/ari_wallach_3_ways_to_plan_for_the_very_long_term

CHAPTER 9

Marsh, Nigel. "How to Make Work-Life Balance Work." Filmed May 2010 in Sydney, Australia. TEDxSydney video, 9:49. https://www.ted.com/talks/nigel_marsh_how_to_make_work_life_balance_work

Moulder, Heather. "10 Reasons Why Work-Life Balance is Important (2021 Edition)." *Inside Out Success (blog)*. *Course Correction Coaching*, Accessed June 6, 2021. https://www.coursecorrectioncoaching.com/reasons-why-work-life-balance-is-important/

Shetty, Jay. "How do I Find Balance in My Life?" October 18, 2019. Video, 3:00. https://www.youtube.com/watch?v=4wiA6zfpP6w

TEDx Talks. "Dan Thurmon: off Balance on Purpose: The Future of Engagement and Work Life Balance." April 15, 2013. Video, 18:07. https://www.youtube.com/watch?v=8OkzozrUEHY

TEDx Talks. "Michael Walters: The Fallacy of the Work/Life Balance." April 10, 2017. Video, 11:19. https://www.youtube.com/watch?v=hJIkgFn2efc

CONCLUSION

Centola, Damon, Joshua Becker, Devon Brackbill, and Andrea Baronchelli. "Experimental Evidence for Tipping Points in Social Convention." *Science* 360, no. 6393 (2018): 1116-1119. https://doi.org/10.1126/science.aas8827

Fleming, Alexander. "On the Antibacterial Action of Cultures of a Penicillium, With Special Reference to Their Use in the Isolation of B. influenzae." *British Journal of Experimental Pathology* 10, no. 3 (June 1929): 226-236. https://www.ncbi.nlm.nih.gov/pmc/articles/PMC2048009/

Kulvaitis, Katie. "Penicillin: An accidental discovery changed the course of medicine." *Healios: EndocrineToday*, August 10, 2008. https://www.healio.com/news/endocrinology/20120325/penicillin-an-accidental-discovery-changed-the-course-of-medicine

Tedx Talks. "Paul Dixon: Adults Let's Have Fun Playing with Your Favorite Childhood Toy." Video, 6:53. June 14, 2018. https://www.youtube.com/watch?v=-Eb_CylV9T4

Tedx Talks. "Starla Fitch: Connect or Die: The Surprising Power of Human Relationships." Video, 12:05. August 25, 2015. youtube.com/watch?v=z-WwsALhH04

Tedx Talks. "Dr. Shelle VanEtten de Sanchez: The Power of Collaboration." Video, 6:29. January 15, 2014. https://www.youtube.com/watch?v=VmQVNE-MbKI

Made in the USA
Monee, IL
08 June 2024

59622899R00098